A Course in Applied Linguistics

Hashim H. Noor & Nassir S. Al-Qadi

A Course in Applied Linguistics

for EFL/ESL Arab Students

PETER LANG

Bern · Berlin · Bruxelles · Frankfurt am Main · New York · Oxford · Wien

Bibliographic information published by die Deutsche Nationalbibliothek
Die Deutsche Nationalbibliothek lists this publication in the Deutsche
Nationalbibliografie; detailed bibliographic data is available on the Internet
at ‹http://dnb.d-nb.de›.

British Library Cataloguing-in-Publication Data: A catalogue record for
this book is available from The British Library, Great Britain

Library of Congress Cataloging-in-Publication Data: 431112

Cover: iStockphoto/Giii

ISBN 978-3-0343-2111-2 pb.   ISBN 978-3-0343-2273-7 eBook
ISBN 978-3-0343-2275-1 MOBI   ISBN 978-3-0343-2274-4 EPUB

© Peter Lang AG, International Academic Publishers, Bern 2016
Hochfeldstrasse 32, CH-3012 Bern, Switzerland
info@peterlang.com, www.peterlang.com

All rights reserved.
All parts of this publication are protected by copyright.
Any utilisation outside the strict limits of the copyright law, without
the permission of the publisher, is forbidden and liable to prosecution.
This applies in particular to reproductions, translations, microfilming,
and storage and processing in electronic retrieval systems.

بسم الله الرحمن الرحيم

"ومن آياته خلق السموات والأرض واختلاف ألسنتكم وألوانكم إن في ذلك لآيات للعالمين"

سورة الروم، آية ٢٣

"And among His signs is the creation of the heavens and the earth, and the difference of your languages and colours. Verily, in that are indeed signs for men of sound knowledge."

Surah 30. Ar-Rum, verse 23

Acknowledgments

We would like to express our deep and sincere gratitude to all those experienced teachers of Linguistics in general and Applied Linguistics in particular who enriched our knowledge with their valuable ideas for developing this book. We must also acknowledge our students who motivated us to generate an Applied Linguistics curriculum that meets the academic needs of native-Arabic speakers learning English as a second/foreign language. Our appreciation is likewise due to all our colleagues at the Department of Languages and Translation, College of Arts and Humanities, Taibah University, Madinah, Saudi Arabia for their encouragement to produce the first edition of this book. Over the last ten years of teaching the first edition, they have continued their support by offering valuable suggestions, which have been implemented into this second edition. We would also like to recognize all textbook writers of Linguistics/Applied Linguistics whose works we benefited from while composing this book.

Our deepest respect and gratitude go to our beloved parents for their love, care, and encouragement (May Allah bless them). Last but not least, our warm love is due to our wives and children for putting up with a great deal during the writing of the book.

Preface

Like other academic domains, every year writers introduce fresh textbooks comprising innovative methods and theories on EFL/ESL teaching all over the world. The latest developed textbooks in any area really help teachers impart knowledge to their students using newly-devised pedagogical trends.

The textbook in hand in its second edition has been specifically developed taking into account the academic needs of undergraduate Arab EFL/ESL students who are prepared as instructors to teach English to native-Arabic speakers at school level. This text is also suitable for graduate Arab EFL/ESL students who have little or no prior knowledge of applied linguistics. It is hoped that the coverage of the theoretical views in L1 and L2 acquisition/learning will be very useful for learners themselves and for future teachers. Also, the knowledge and learning insights gained from the experience of their teachers may facilitate their practice of new dimensions in classroom methodology.

This textbook in its second edition is an outcome of more than twenty years of professional collaboration. Throughout this period, we have been teaching *language* courses and *Introduction to Linguistics*, *Applied Linguistics*, and *Linguistics* courses to Arab EFL students at Taibah University in Madinah, KSA. Our practical experience and discussions with linguistics/applied linguistics experts have helped us develop our ideas about the correlation between language acquisition research and classroom practice, especially with Arab EFL students.

Chapter 1 begins with a controversial issue, i.e. what is applied linguistics? To answer this question, theoretical views and premises of various linguists are discussed. An effort is made to define the term "applied linguistics" as a discipline, quoting observations of experts in linguistics and applied linguistics. The areas and role of this discipline are examined briefly.

Chapter 2 discusses how children acquire their first language. The views of prominent theorists and psychologists regarding common approaches of first language acquisition are discussed by surveying recent works on L1 acquisition. The opinions of four main theorists, i.e. behaviorists, innatists, cognitists and interactionists, are accurately reviewed.

Chapter 3 includes several theories concerning Second Language Acquisition (SLA). In addition to the study of SLA in its historical perspective, four main theoretical concepts and approaches: the Behavioristic Approach, the Cognitive or Psychological Approach, the Creative Construction Approach and the Sociological Approach, are critically evaluated. Questions such as: How important are imitation and practice for language learning? and To what extent can theories of acquiring a first language be applied to second/foreign language learning? are precisely answered.

Chapter 4 reviews three approaches regarding learners' performance, i.e. Contrastive Analysis (CA), Error Analysis (EA) and Interlanguage (IL). As errors are generally considered important determinants of the SLA process, an effort is made to answer the following questions: (1) What are the errors committed by L2 learners and what are their characteristics? (2) What are the causes of these errors? and (3) What is the role of these errors in learning and teaching an L2? Provided are opportunities for students to compare some aspects of two languages (Arabic and English) and analyze errors of selected Arab EFL students' performance.

Chapter 5 deals with the most common non-linguistic factors, like aptitude, intelligence, motivation, anxiety, and personality that affect SLA. These intrinsic and extrinsic factors play a vital role in affecting learners' pace of SLA. Views and observations of various psychologists and linguistics experts are discussed in this respect.

Chapter 6 discusses the common language learning strategies that help Arab EFL/ESL students overcome learning problems. Characteristics and types of learning strategies are discussed as well. Moreover, the factors that affect strategy choice are also given due consideration. Finally, views of researchers regarding the effect of strategy training in language teaching are also discussed.

To make this book more fruitful for its readers, each chapter is followed by study questions, suggestions for further reading and practical projects. The authors hope that EFL/ESL teachers find it as a useful resource to aid in classroom instruction. Finally, the authors hope that applied linguistics researchers find it as a viable source of language learning approaches, features of learners' performance, non-linguistic factors that influence L1 and L2 acquisition, and language learning strategies.

Contents

Acknowledgments 7

Preface 9

Chapter 1: What Is Applied Linguistics? 17
   1.1   Introduction 17
   1.2   Definitions of the Term 18
   1.3   Areas of Applied Linguistics 20
          1.3.1   Language Teaching and Learning 20
          1.3.2   Language Policy and Language Planning 21
          1.3.3   Speech Therapy/Pathology 21
          1.3.4   Lexicography and Dictionary Making 22
          1.3.5   Translation and Interpretation 23
          1.3.6   Computer assisted Language
                  Learning/Instruction 23
   1.4   Conclusion 24
   Study Questions 25
   For Further Reading 26
   References 27

Chapter 2: First Language Acquisition 29
   2.1   Introduction 29
   2.2   The Outlook of Behaviorists/Environmentalists 30
   2.3   The Views of Innatists/Nativists 33
   2.4   The Viewpoint of Cognitists 35
   2.5   The Viewpoint of Interactionists 36
   2.6   Conclusion 38

	Study Questions	38
	Projects	39
	For Further Reading	40
	References	41

Chapter 3: Second Language Acquisition 43
   3.1   Introduction 43
   3.2   Historical Perspective 45
   3.3   Behavioristic Approach 47
         3.3.1   Critical Evaluation of the Behavioristic Approach 48
   3.4   Cognitive/Psychological Approach 49
   3.5   Creative Construction Approach 51
         3.5.1   The Acquisition-Learning Hypothesis 54
         3.5.2   The Monitor Hypothesis 55
         3.5.3   The Natural-order Hypothesis 56
         3.5.4   The Input Hypothesis 56
         3.5.5   The Affective-filter Hypothesis 57
   3.6   Sociological Approach 58
   3.7   Conclusion 60
   Study Questions 60
   Projects 61
   For Further Reading 62
   References 64

Chapter 4: Approaches To Learners' Performance 69
   4.1   Introduction 69
   4.2   Contrastive Analysis (CA) 70
         4.2.1   The Rationale of CA 71
         4.2.2   Factors of Negative Transfer 72
         4.2.3   CA Assumptions 73
         4.2.4   CA Hierarchy of Difficulty 73
         4.2.5   CA Methodology 75
         4.2.6   CA Technique: An example 76
         4.2.7   CA and L2 Teaching 77

      4.2.8   CA Critics 78
      4.2.9   CA Defense 78
  4.3   Error Analysis (EA) 80
      4.3.1   The Importance of EA 81
      4.3.2   EA and CA Differences 81
      4.3.3   EA Methodology 81
      4.3.4   EA Critics 83
  4.4   Interlanguage (IL) 84
      4.4.1   IL Assumptions 85
      4.4.2   Cognitive Processes of IL 85
      4.4.3   IL and Similarities with Natural Languages 86
      4.4.4   IL and Natural Differences in Languages 86
      4.4.5   IL Methodology 87
      4.4.6   IL and L2 Teaching 87
      4.4.7   IL Critics 88
  4.5   Conclusion 88
  Study Questions 89
  Projects 90
  For Further Reading 91
  References 93

Chapter 5: Non-Linguistic Factors In L2 Learning 97
  5.1   Introduction 97
  5.2   Language Aptitude 98
  5.3   Intelligence 99
  5.4   Motivation 100
      5.4.1   Factors Affecting Motivation 101
  5.5   Anxiety 101
  5.6   Personality 102
  5.7   Age 103
  5.8   Conclusion 105
  Study Questions 105
  Projects 106
  For Further Reading 107
  References 108

Chapter 6: Language Learning Strategies 111
   6.1   Introduction 111
   6.2   Definitions of Learning Strategies.................................... 112
   6.3   Characteristics of Language Learning Strategies 114
   6.4   Types of Language Learning Strategies 115
       6.4.1   O'Malley et al.'s Framework 115
       6.4.2   Oxford's Classification.. 118
   6.5   Factors Affecting Strategy Choice 120
       6.5.1   Age... 120
       6.5.2   Aptitude 120
       6.5.3   Motivation... 121
       6.5.4   Personality... 121
       6.5.5   The Learner's Personal Background 121
       6.5.6   Situational and Social Factors............................. 122
   6.6   The Strategies of Good Language Learners 122
   6.7   Language Learning Strategies & Language Teaching..... 124
   6.8   Conclusion 125
   Study Questions 125
   Projects... 126
   For Further Reading 127
   References.. 128

Glossary 131

Appendix... 145

Chapter 1: What Is Applied Linguistics?

This is an introductory chapter that deals with the following points:

1. Definitions of the term *Applied Linguistics* (AL).
2. Areas of AL:
   a. Language teaching and learning
   b. Language policy and language planning
   c. Speech therapy/pathology
   d. Lexicography and dictionary making
   e. Translation and interpretation
   f. Computer assisted language learning/ instruction

1.1 Introduction

The term applied linguistics (AL) is an Anglo-American coinage. As Strevens (1992:13) testifies, the term came to be used coincidentally both in Britain and in the United States of America. It has been in use in Britain since the establishment of the University of Edinburgh's School of Applied Linguistics in 1956, and in the United States of America, since the establishment of the Center of Applied Linguistics in Washington, D.C. in 1957. According to Mackey (1966:197), its use was promulgated by those who clearly wanted to be known as scientists and not as humanists because scientists had brought about much greater technological progress than humanists at that time. By applying linguistics, it was thought that the scientific status of the natural sciences would be conferred upon linguistics as well.

AL has, in the past, sometimes based itself solely on the findings of theoretical linguistics. The position then was, essentially, that in order to be able to teach a language, one needed to know how the language in question was structured (e.g. grammar and translation, and audio-lingual methods of language teaching were very common). Within foreign language teaching, it was especially linguists who had contributed so greatly to the language courses that had been designed for the US army during World War II. Contrary to this assumption, a large number of authors of the last few decades have expressed their conviction that there was more than one discipline as the basis of foreign/second language teaching or learning. In addition to linguistics and its sub-disciplines, one often finds related fields like psychology, sociology, pedagogy, and education.

The purpose of AL is to investigate problems related to language teaching and learning and to take some practical steps to solve these problems. AL originated in language education – first-language, second-language and foreign-language teaching and learning – but is now also an integral part of various specialized fields such as speech therapy, lexicography and dictionary making, translation and interpretation, etc.

1.2 Definitions of the Term

In order to define the term "applied linguistics", two main questions should be answered: First, what branch of linguistics can be applied to the real-world language-based problems that AL presumes to mediate? Second, what kinds of problems can be solved through the mediation of AL? Arguing in depth about these two questions is well beyond the scope of this book. One can argue here that AL uses information taken from the social-scientific disciplines including linguistics to solve these problems. Unlike general linguistics, AL does not regard language as an isolated subject to be examined away from its social environment (Kaplan & Grabe, 1992). What is applied must concern itself with language because it is a central component which Corder (1974) spells out by saying:

> "Applied linguistics is [...] the utilization of the knowledge about the nature of language achieved by linguistic research for the improvement of the efficiency of some practical task in which language is a central component."

Crystal (1985:19), however, indicates that AL is a branch of linguistics:

> "[...] where the primary concern is the application of linguistic theories, methods and findings to the elucidation of language problems which have arisen in other areas of experience."

The main concern of AL is the teaching and learning of foreign/second languages, and sometimes the term, AL, is used as if this were the only field involved.

Richards et al. (1985:15) maintain that AL covers two main points:

> "1) the study of second and foreign language learning and teaching,
> 2) the study of language and linguistics in relation to practical problems, such as lexicography, translation, speech pathology, etc."

In order to develop its own theoretical models of language and language use, AL takes information from psychology, sociology, anthropology, and information theory, as well as from linguistics. It then uses this information and theory in practical areas like syllabus design, speech therapy, language planning, stylistics, educational linguistics, etc.

For a short working definition of the discipline, one can use Strevens' (1992) definition, which says that:

> "applied linguistics is a multidisciplinary approach to the solution of language-related problems" (p.17).

Wilkins (1999:7), however, shows the purposes of AL in the following definition:

> "In a broad sense, applied linguistics is concerned with increasing understanding of the role of language in human affairs and thereby with providing the knowledge necessary for those who are responsible for taking language-related decisions

whether the need for these arises in the classroom, the workplace, regarding laws, in the court, or in the laboratory."

From these definitions of the term AL, it is evident that it covers, in addition to language teaching and language learning (of first and second languages), several areas of language studies, ranging from language disorders, language therapy, lexicography, translation, professional uses of language, etc.

1.3 Areas of Applied Linguistics

As we have seen from the definitions of AL, this discipline covers areas of language teaching and learning of second or foreign languages, speech therapy, lexicography and dictionary making, translation and interpretation, to mention only a few. It seems appropriate then to explain these areas of AL in brief:

1.3.1 Language Teaching and Learning

It is generally accepted that AL is not the only source of advancement in language teaching and learning. Pedagogy, psychology, psycholinguistics and linguistics also deal somewhat with language teaching and learning. Today, AL can be seen as providing the intellectual basis for advances in language teaching and learning in numerous contexts in a number of countries. However, the relation between AL and language teaching and learning is indirect. AL does not take developments in linguistics and look for ways of applying them to teaching and learning. Instead, the problems faced in language teaching and learning are solved with the help of linguistics (Wilkins, 1972:228). For example, when a language teacher faces a problem in presenting linguistic points (e.g. the Present Simple Tense in English), he often finds himself referring back to linguistic description[1] to see if there is something he has overlooked. He may even check certain aspects of the target language against similar features of the learner's mother-tongue to see how he can best take advantage of these commonalities.

1.3.2 Language Policy and Language Planning

AL has often been a great source of minimizing complex social, political, economic, linguistic, and cultural tensions, especially those in situations such as large-scale population movement, refugee flow, the attainment of political independence, and similar events. AL also plays a vital role in planning the national or local language(s) of concerned countries (e.g. ways of spreading the use of a language, spelling reforms, or the addition of new words to the language). In Indonesia, for example, Malay was chosen as the national language and was given the name Bahasa Indonesia (Indonesian Language). It became the primary language of education (Richards, et al 1985:158). AL assists language planners by providing answers to questions like: To whom does the policy/ plan apply: the entire school-aged population, or some particular segment of that population? It also seeks to know at what level the policy or plan applies: elementary, secondary, and/or higher education, etc.

1.3.3 Speech Therapy/Pathology

Speech therapy/pathology or clinical linguistics includes activities and exercises designed to help relieve or overcome language problems or speech defects (e.g. stuttering) or to help someone regain the use of speech after having suffered speech loss (Richards et al, 1985:268). In recent years, a revolution has taken place through the incorporation of AL into many professional training courses for treating patients with speech disorders by speech therapists (or speech-language pathologists).

---

1   Linguistic description refers to phonological, morphlogical, syntactic or semantic analysis or features of the language to be taught.

In addition, both psycholinguists[2] and neurolinguists[3] have been working to find out how language develops in the brain, and how brain injuries affect both language memory and language production. A better understanding of how language is processed will assist in overcoming such speech disorders. A number of clinics and research labs attached to departments of linguistics and applied linguistics in various universities (especially in Britain and United States of America) were found to help treat speech disorders (such as aphasia[4] and stuttering) or problems in speech production (e.g. tongue-slip and hesitation).

1.3.4 Lexicography and Dictionary Making

Technological developments in printing and publishing have made dictionary making a much more rapid process. This may also be due to the creation and harmonization of terminology and to large-scale library database networks that are now spreading throughout the world (Kaplan, 1983). A new generation of lexicographers has emerged whose loyalty lie with linguistics. These new lexicographers are in fact engaged in AL for at least part of their task. Sinclair's (1987) Cobuild Dictionary is a principal example of the way applied linguists contribute to lexicography. This dictionary is a computerized database designed to link the learning of vocabulary thematically to real-world communicative contexts.

---

2   Psycholinguists study the correlation between linguistic behavior and the psychological processes that underlie that behavior.
3   Neurolinguists study the neurological development of man and attempt to construct a model of the brain's control over the processes of speech and hearing. They also study the function the brain performs in language use. Psycholinguistics and neurolinguistics are two different fields of linguistics.
4   Aphasia is the loss of ability to use speech or understand speech as a result of brain injury.

1.3.5 Translation and Interpretation

The translation and interpretation of texts and speeches, without human intervention, still remain an intangible goal. This may be due to a number of factors: the influence of the context, irony and the use of idioms, the constant creation of original metaphors, and the fact that some semantic ambiguity is inherent in natural languages. The task of attaining further improvement towards success is shared by both computer engineers and applied linguists. The training of translators and interpreters now often includes training in AL (specifically, in the area of Contrastive Analysis where the translator is trained to point out the areas of similarities and differences between the languages concerned).[5]

1.3.6 Computer assisted Language Learning/Instruction

By the mid-1980's, microcomputers had been around long enough for many people to have had sufficient contact with them to recognize their potential as a tool for language teachers and learners. Many computer programs and specific software were developed to assist in learning and teaching languages. Computer-Assisted-Language-Learning (CALL) and Computer-Assisted-Language-Instruction (CALI) had emerged, the purpose of which was to take advantage of this technology in the fields of learning and teaching languages (Pennington and Stevens, 1994). These may include:

a) A Teaching program
   This teaching program is presented by a computer in a sequence. The student responds on the computer, and the computer indicates whether the responses are correct or incorrect.
b) Monitoring students' progress
   The computer is used to monitor students' progress and direct them to the appropriate lessons, material, etc.

---

5   See 4.2 for the discussion of Contrastive Analysis.

c) Providing exploratory environments
   The computer is used to provide exploratory environments for language learning by presenting problems in need of resolution, and providing tools for further work and learning.

1.4 Conclusion

We have so far discussed only some of the applications of the findings of AL in relation to other sciences like psychology, education, medicine, etc. In addition, there are other applications of the findings of AL in law (e.g. the patterns and implications of co-speech in legal settings, the treatment of language disorders, the grammar of a lie), and in business (e.g. linguistic advertising, foreign language applications in business) (Di Pietro, ed., 1982; Penman, 1987).

AL, as basically the study of second and foreign language learning and acquisition, centers on the learner as the central point of the learning process. Many recent studies and research in this area concentrate more on the learner with respect to his acquisition of a foreign language, his behavior, how he processes the language, his errors, his attitude and aptitude, and his motivation for learning the language, etc. (see Figure 1.1).

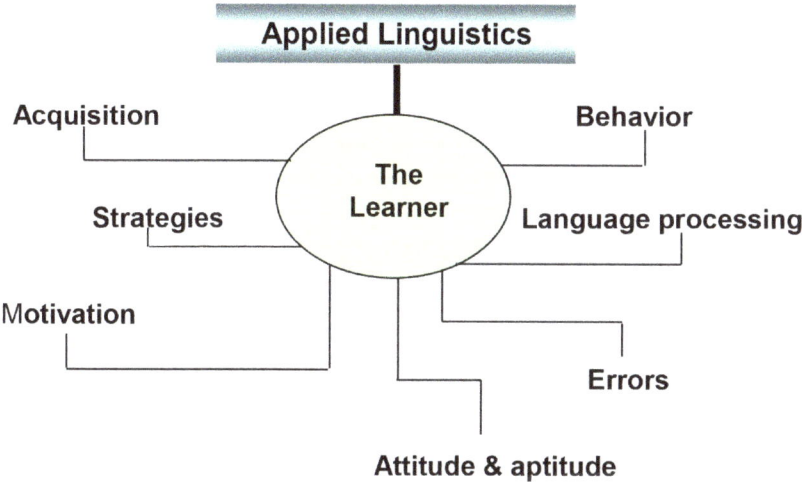

Figure 1.1: The learner, the focus of AL.

In the following chapters, we will see how the learner acquires his native language, which is usually referred to as the first language (L1) and how this acquisition affects his learning an additional language, which is usually referred to as a second language (L2). We will also see why he commits errors and what the reasons are behind these errors. The non-linguistic factors that affect his language development and the strategies he follows to acquire the second language will also be covered.

Study Questions

1. Why is the term AL an Anglo-American coinage?
2. In the past, why did AL base itself on the findings of theoretical linguistics?

3. When was the term AL first used in Britain and in the United States of America?
4. What is the definition of the term AL, as mentioned in the text, that takes into account real-world language-based problems?
5. What are other disciplines in addition to linguistics and its sub-disciplines that form the basis of foreign language teaching and learning?
6. What is the main concern of AL?
7. Give a short definition of the term AL.
8. What are other areas that AL covers besides the teaching and learning of foreign/second languages?
9. How can AL help in solving problems that arise in the area of language teaching and learning?
10. How can computers assist 'language instruction' and 'language learning'?

For Further Reading

For a more complete introductory account of views on the definitions of applied linguistics, the books of Robert Kaplan (1980), Peter Strevens (1992), and Norbert Schmitt (ed.) (2002) provide an accessible treatment. A full account of the domains of the discipline can also be found in Kaplan (1980). And the more technical accounts of applied linguistics and language teaching and learning are featured in Chapter 8 of Wilkins (1972), Chapter 7 of Corder (1973), and Howatt (1984). Volume 14 of the Annual Review of Applied Linguistics (1993/94) provides a thorough up-to-date discussion of views on language policy and planning. In-depth treatment of speech-therapy can be found in Jackson (1989) and Fletcher (1990). For a broad discussion of lexicography and dictionary making, see Hartmann (1985). Pennington and Stevens' (1994) collection of papers gives an excellent description of computer applications in applied linguistics, and second/foreign language teaching.

References

Corder, S.P. 1973. *Introducing Applied Linguistics*. Middlesex: Penguin Books.
Corder, S.P. 1974. Problems and solutions in applied linguistics, in J. et al. Qvistgaard *Applied Linguistics: Problems and Solutions*, Heildlberg, 3–23.
Crystal, D. 1985. *A Dictionary of Linguistics and Phonetics*. London: Basil Blackwell.
Di Pietro, R. (Ed.) 1982. *Linguistics and the Professions*. Proceedings of the Second Annual Delaware Symposium on Language Studies. New Jersey: Ablex Publishing Corporation.
Fletcher, P. 1990. Language pathology. In R. Kaplan et al. (eds.), *Annual Review of Applied Linguistics* (1989), Vol. 10, New York: Cambridge University Press, 26–36.
Grabe, W. (Ed.) 1993/94. *Annual Review of Applied Linguistics*. New York: Cambridge University Press.
Grishman, R. 1986. *Computational linguistics: An introduction.* Cambridge: Cambridge University Press.
Hartmann, R. R. 1985. Lexicography: A contrastive survey. In R. Kaplan et al. (eds.), *Annual Review of Applied Linguistics* (1984), Vol. 5, New York: Cambridge University Press, 125–38.
Howatt, A. P. 1984. *A History of English Language Teaching*. New York: Oxford University Press.
Jackson, C. A. 1989. Linguistics and speech-language pathology. In F. Newmeyer (Ed.), *Linguistics: The Cambridge Survey*. Vol. 3, Cambridge: Cambridge University Press.
Johnson, K. & Johnson, H. (Eds.) 1998. *Encyclopedic Dictionary of Applied Linguistics,* Hong Kong, Blackwell.
Kaplan, R. B. (Ed.) 1980. *On the Scope of Applied Linguistics*. Rowley, MA: Newbury House.
Kaplan, R. B. 2002. *The Oxford Handbook of Applied Linguistics*. OUP.
Kaplan, R. B. & W. Grabe 1992. *Introduction to Applied Linguistics.* Reading: Addison-Wesley,

Mackey, W. 1966. Applied linguistics: its meaning and use, *English Language Teaching.* 20:197–206.

McDonough, S. 2002 *Applied Linguistics in Language Education*, London, Arnold.

Penman, R. 1987. Discourse in courts: Cooperation, coercion, and coherence. *Discourse Processes* 10/3:201–8.

Pennington, M. C. & Stevens, V. (Eds.) 1994. *Computers in Applied Linguistics.* Clevedon: Multilingual Matters.

Richards, J., Platt, J. and Weber, H. 1985. Longman Dictionary of Applied Linguistics. Suffolk: Longman.

Schmitt, N. (Ed.) 2002. *An Introduction to Applied Linguistics.* London, Arnold.

Sinclair, J. (Ed.) 1987. *Looking up: An Account of the COBUILD Project.* London: Collins ELT.

Strevens, P. 1992. Applied linguistics: An overview. In W. Grabe & R. Kaplan, *Introduction to Applied Linguistics.* Reading: Addison-Wesley, 13–34.

Wilkins, D. A. 1972. *Linguistics in Language Teaching.* London: Edward Arnold.

Wilkins, D. A. 1999 Applied linguistics. In Splosky, B. (ed.) *Concise Encyclopedia of Educational Linguistics.* Amsterdam: Elsevier; 6–17.

Chapter 2: First Language Acquisition

This chapter discusses how children acquire their first language. It covers the following approaches of first langauge acquisition:

1. Behavioristic Approach
2. Innatist/Nativistic Approach
3. Cognitive/Psychological Approach
4. Interactionist Approach

2.1 Introduction

One of the most fascinating aspects of human development is the ability to acquire a language. We all watch and listen with absolute fascination to the first words uttered by babies. Indeed, learning a language is an amazing achievement which has attracted the attention of linguists and psycholinguists for generations. It is believed, with complete confidence, that human language is a gift from our Creator, Allah, for all mankind. To that end, human beings are provided with certain biological tools, which enable us to acquire language proficiency from infancy. In this regard, there are certain questions that need to be tackled:

1. How can children make use of these tools in order to comprehend and produce the language?
2. What is it that enables a child not only to acquire words, but to put them together into meaningful sentences?
3. What motivates and enables children to continue developing complex grammatical structures, even though their early communication is successful for all intents and purposes?

These are only some questions regarding language acquisition.

In this chapter, we will discuss several ideas and approaches to answer the aforementioned questions and many others. Four main views regarding first language acquisition will be discussed: the behaviorist (or the environmentalist), the innatist, the cognitist and the interactionist.

2.2 The Outlook of Behaviorists/Environmentalists

Before the 1960s, the study of child language was dominated mainly by the 'behavioristic' approach to language acquisition. The best-known proponent of this approach was B. F. Skinner (1957). Skinner put rats into a cage with two levers and if the rat pressed the first lever, a morsel of food would fall into the cage. If the rat pressed the second lever, it would get itching powder thrown over it. It proved that rats are capable of learning; and after a number of tries they systematically pressed the first lever. On the basis of this type of animal behavior, Skinner defined the notion of reinforcement. He speaks of positive and negative reinforcement as:

Positive reinforcement is an increase in the possibility of occurrence of a response to a stimulus, since this correct response is rewarded.

Negative reinforcement is a decrease in the possibility of occurrence of a response to a stimulus, since this wrong response is punished.

From the observation of systematization and prediction of animal responses to stimuli in laboratory experiments, Skinner wanted to draw conclusions about human behavior.

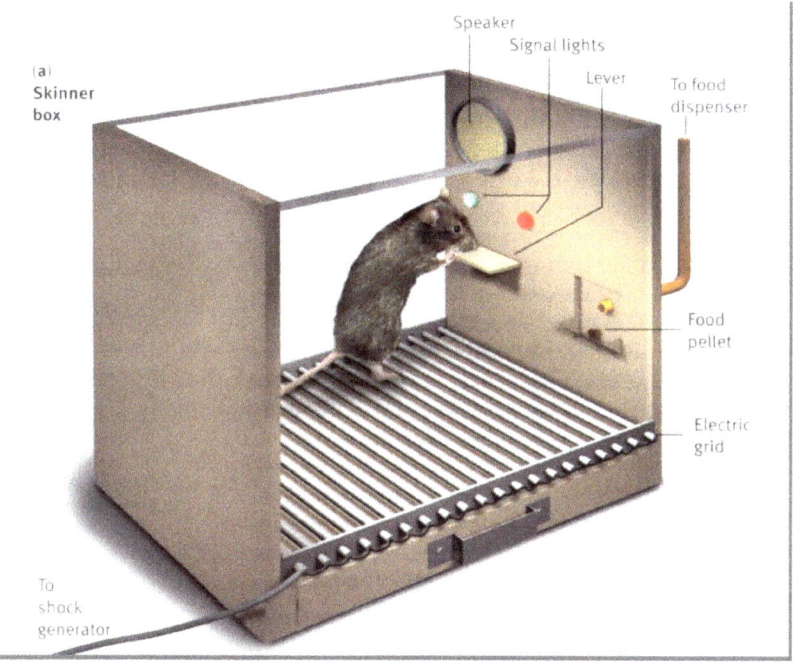

Figure 2.1: Reinforcement inside a cage: Skinner's experiment.

To Skinner, a theory of language acquisition should be derived from the general behaviorist acquisition theory, which indicates that language learning is simply a matter of imitation and habit-formation. Children imitate the sounds and patterns which they hear around them and receive positive reinforcement (by rewards or approval or just successful communication) for doing so. With the encouragement of those in the environment around them, children continue to imitate and practice these sounds and patterns until they form 'habits' of correct language use. The quality and quantity of language which the child hears, as well as consistency of reinforcement offered by the environment, have an effect on the child's success in first language acquisition. Within this framework, a child's 'errors' are simply considered the result of imperfect acquisition.

Criticism of the behaviorists

In recent years, it has become clear that this principle does not explain all the facts of language acquisition and development. Children imitate a great deal, especially in acquiring sounds and vocabulary, but little of their grammatical ability can be explained in this way. Two types of evidence are commonly produced in support of this remark:

1. *The kind of language children produce*: They say, for example, *goed* and *taked* (for the irregular Past-Tense forms) instead of *went* and *took* or they say *mouses* and *sheeps* (for the plural forms) instead of *mice* and *sheep*. This is generally called an overgeneralization process or strategy children use in the langauge process.
2. What *They do not produce*: In the following dialogue, for example, a child proved unable to use a pattern even though the parent presented the correct adult model several times:

CHILD:	*Nobody don't like me.
MOTHER:	No, say 'Nobody likes me'.
	(Eight repetitions of this dialogue).
CHILD:	*Oh! Nobody don't likes me.
	(McNeill (1933) cited in Crystal, 1987:234)

The errors mentioned in these examples, along with other similar ones, triggered the attention of scholars to the processes of first language acquisition. Imitation and reinforcement, or practice alone cannot explain such errors since the forms created by the child were never produced by adults. Rather, children appear to discern patterns and then generalize them in new contexts (e.g. *taked* and *sheeps*).

2.3 The Views of Innatists/Nativists

The Innatists or Nativists maintain that first language acquisition is not simply a matter of imitation/reinforcement. It is rather a complex system of rules which enables the child to understand and create an infinite number of sentences. This creativity of the child is apparent in the extraction of abstract knowledge in the form of rules from concrete examples. Children seem to construct their own rule-systems, which they gradually adapt in the direction of the adult system. The innatists or nativists argue that children are born with a language faculty (innate ability) which is already equipped with considerable knowledge about the form that human language takes, and have only to be exposed to particular human languages for their mental grammars to be fixed in appropriate ways. This phenomenon happens since certain general principles for discovering or structuring language automatically begin to operate when children are exposed to this language. These principles constitute a child's 'language acquisition device' (LAD).

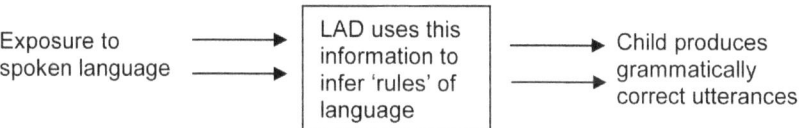

Figure 2.2: Child's Language Acquisition Device (LAD).

The child uses his LAD to make sense of the utterances heard around him, deriving from this adult speech or 'primary linguistic data' hypotheses about the grammar of the language – what sentences are, and how they are constructed, etc. The knowledge, which is derived from these hypotheses, is then used to produce sentences that, after a process of trial and error, correspond to those in adult speech. This makes the child learn a set of generalizations, or rules, governing the way the sentences are formed.

Eric Lenneberg, a psycholinguist (1967), compares learning to talk with learning to walk. He argues that the LAD, like other biological functions, works successfully only when it is stimulated at the right time – a time which is referred to as the 'critical period'. This critical period lasts till puberty (i.e. around the age of 12 or 13 years), and is a factor of biological development. Lenneberg is of the opinion that language acquisition may be more difficult after puberty because the brain loses the ability of adaptation.

The notion that there is a specific and limited timeperiod for language acquisition is referred to as the Critical Period Hypothesis. The best evidence in support of this hypothesis is that every child virtually learns language on a schedule, which is very similar to other children in spite of quite different life circumstances.

In more recent writings, Chomsky and his followers no longer use the term LAD, but refer to the child's innate endowment as "universal grammar" (UG). UG is the system of categories, operations, and principles shared by all human languages and is considered to be innate. It is considered to consist of a set of principles which are common to all languages. Children who are pre-equipped with UG have to learn the ways in which their own language makes use of these principles and the variations which may exist in the particular language that these children are learning (Chomsky, 1981; Cook, 1996; White 1989).

However, there are some phenomena in L1 acquisition and development that should be explained. There is, for example, the remarkable speed with which children learn to speak and their similarities in the way they acquire grammatical patterns in different languages. Also, regularities of language, which children work out for themselves, cannot only be referred to as 'primary linguistic data' (i.e., adult speech), because this speech is too complex and disorganized. These types of phenomena led people to think of the role of cognition in the development of language.

2.4 The Viewpoint of Cognitists

According to cognitists, first language acquisition must be viewed within the context of a child's intellectual (i.e. mental and linguistic) growth. Knowledge of language grows as the child's mental (or cognitive) abilities grow. This happens as a result of the child's interaction with his or her environment. Linguistic structures will emerge in the child's language only if there is an already-established cognitive foundation. This means that less complex structures appear (acquired) earlier in the language of the child than more complex structures. For example, Cromer (1974) found that the Present Perfect Tense in English (e.g. He has gone.) was not used before the age of four and a half despite the fact that the form was frequent in parents' speech. He examined other aspects of children's speech and found that the Present Perfect Tense did not appear until they had acquired the underlying concept of 'present relevance'. It was found that the children used the Present Simple and Present Continuous forms (e.g. 'Here's the cat.' and 'I'm coming.') before they started using the Present Perfect Tense.

The cognitists are of the view that children, in the process of language development, follow a number of *'operating principles'* or strategies in making sense of language data. Slobin (1973), on the basis of data from a large number of unrelated languages, has formulated these principles which were later manifested by Clark and Clark (1977) as follows:

1) *Avoid exceptions:*
   This principle accounts for the overgeneralization process and is demonstrated in morphological development. Children produce *breaked, mouses, mans*, etc., for *broke, mice, men*. This proves that regular rules are acquired and developed before irregular ones.
2) *Clear meaning-relationships of words:*
   The underlying meaning-relationships of words should be clearly marked in the mind of children. This might explain why the Active Voice appears before the Passive Voice in the course of language development of children:

[1] The student handed the exam paper to the teacher.
[2] The exam paper was handed to the teacher.

There seems to be a natural tendency to prefer the first noun in a sentence as the subject (the student in [1]) and the second, as the object (the teacher [2]). This shows why the *Active* is easier than the *Passive*.

3) *Semantic sense of grammatical markers:*

Children tend to use grammatical markers (such as *am, is, are, a, an, this, there, in,* etc.) in order to make sense of the patterns they hear. This may account for the late acquisition of Ø-marked adult categories. For example, forms which may undergo contraction or deletion tend to be initially absent in children's speech as in *I will* before *I'll,* and *The pen which he used* before *The pen he used*.

In sum, the study of such operating principles or strategies may lead to a better understanding of what is easy or difficult for L1 learners.

2.5 The Viewpoint of Interactionists

The interactionists are of the opinion that language develops as a result of the complex interplay between the uniquely human characteristics of the child and the environment in which he grows.

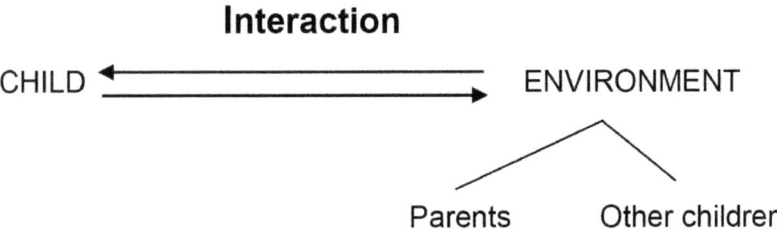

Figure 2.3: First Language Acquisition as Interaction.

There have been a number of observational studies on language in which mothers addressed small children, other adults or older children. These studies of 'motherese', as it came to be called in the 1970's, showed that maternal input is by no means as complex and fragmentary as proponents of the Innateness Theory claimed it to be. Many parents do not talk to their children in the same way as they talk to other adults. Rather, they seem capable of adapting their language to provide the child with the maximum opportunity to interact and learn. These studies have shown that this adaptation, or so-called *'caretaker talk'* or *'speech'*, has a number of characteristics which distinguish it from typical speech between adults. These characteristics are as follows:

1- It is generally spoken more slowly and clearly.
2- It contains shorter utterances. One study showed that the average length of maternal sentences to 2-year-olds was less than four words. In contrast, the study also showed that the number of words of the mothers' utterances to other adults was 8 words.
3- The utterances are considerably simplified, especially with respect to grammar and meaning, with fewer broken sentences or false starts.
4- It contains fewer complex sentences. Sentence 'frames' such as: *Where's [...]?* or *That's [...]* are commonly used by parents.
5- There is less variety of tenses.
6- The range of vocabulary is more limited. The meanings are chiefly 'concrete', relating to present situations in which the mother and the child interact with each other.
7- There are also several features, the purpose of which seems to be clarification. For example, information is provided that would be considered unnecessary when talking to other adults. Sentences may also be repeated several times.

Caretaker talk or *speech* seems particularly well-suited to enable the child to learn the rules and meanings of language. It is clearer to perceive and simpler in structure. The child, by interacting with the parents or other children, has time to become familiar with a limited range of language. One-to-one interaction gives the child access to language which is adjusted to his level of comprehension. When a child does not understand, the adult may repeat or paraphrase. The response of the adult also allows children to know when their own utterances are understood.

2.6 Conclusion

In this chapter, we have surveyed some recent research in L1 acquisition. We have seen how the emphasis of the behaviorists on habit-formation has given way to a more mentally oriented approach, which stresses the child's active contribution to the acquisition process. This process of 'creative construction' seems to lead all children through similar stages of development. There also appears to be fruitful interaction between children's linguistic and cognitive development. Finally, we have seen how the particular language environment of the child seems well-adapted in assisting the acquisition process.

One way of reconciling the views of the behaviorists, innatists, cognitists, and interactionists is to see how each view may help to explain a different aspect of children's language development. In Chapter 3, we will begin to look at the acquisition of second languages by children and older learners. We will see that many of the issues raised in this chapter will be relevant to our discussion of second language acquisition, as well.

Study Questions

1. What is the human being provided with in order to acquire language from very early childhood?
2. To Skinner, a theory of language acquisition should be derived from a general behavioristic learning approach. Briefly discuss.

3. Explain how the behavioristic approach does not explain all the facts of language acquisition and development.
4. According to the *innatists'* view of language acquisition, the child is creative in acquiring his native language. Explain in brief.
5. What do LAD and UG mean? Support your answer with examples.
6. According to the *cognitists'* approach, linguistic structures will emerge in the children's performance only if there is an already-established cognitive foundation. Discuss with examples.
7. What is the difference in the *innatists'* and the *cognitists'* views?
8. What are the three 'operative principles' that children have for making sense of language data in the process of L1 development.
9. 'Caretaker talk/speech seems well suited in helping a child to learn the rules and meanings of the language'. Briefly discuss this notion.

Projects

1. From the thoughts and approaches of first language acquisition you have studied here, give a comprehensive view of how the first language is acquired.
2. Four approaches to first language acquisition have been mentioned in this chapter. Conduct research on the Internet in this field and present one approach which has not been discussed here.
3. Search the Internet for Universal Grammar (UG) and its relation to first language acquisition.

For Further Reading

General Accounts Of First Language Acquisition

Baron, N. 1992. *Growing Up with Language*. Reading, Mass: Addison Wesley.
Clark, E. 2009. *First Language Acquisition*. Cambridge University Press.
Hoff, E. 2008. *Language development*, 4th ed. Farmington Hills, MI: Wadsworth.
Ingram, D. 1989. *First Language Acquisition: Methods, Description and Explanation*. Cambridge University Press.

Chomsky's Innatist Ideas

Chomsky, N. 1959. Review of verbal behavior by B. F. Skinner. *Language* 35:26–58.
Chomsky, N. 1981. *Lectures on Government and Binding*. Dordecht: Foris. Chapter 1.
Cook, V. 2007. Chomsky's *Universal Grammar: An Introduction*. 3rd Edition, Massachusetts: Wiley-Blackwell Publishers Inc.
Singleton and Ryan. 2004. *Language Acquisition: The Age Factor*. 2nd Edition. Cromwell Press Ltd.
White, L. and Newson, M. 1989. *Universal Grammar and Second Language Acquisition*. Amsterdam/Philadelphia, PA: John Benjamins.

Cognitists Ideas

Clark, H. and Clark, E. 1977. *Psychology and Language: An Introduction to Psycholinguistics*. New York.
Foss, B. (Ed.) 1974. *New Perspectives in Child Development*. Harmondsworth: Penguin Books.

Ferguson, C. and Slobin, D. 1973. *Studies of Child Language Development.* New York.

Thorndike, E. L. 1999 [1913], *Education Psychology: briefer course*, New York: Rutledge.

Interactionist Views

Snow, C. E. and Ferguson, C. A. (eds.) 1977. *Talking to children: Language Input and Acquisition.* Cambridge University Press.

References

Baron, N. 1992. *Growing Up with Language.* Reading, Mass: Addison Wesley.

Chomsky, N. 1959. Review of verbal behavior by B. F. Skinner. *Language* 35:26–58.

Chomsky, N. 1981. *Lectures on Government and Binding.* Dordecht: Foris. Chapter 1.

Clark, H. and Clark, E. 1977. *Psychology and Language: An Introduction to Psycholinguistics.* New York.

Cook, V. 1996. Chomsky's *Universal Grammar: An Introduction.* Cambridge, Massachusetts: Blackwell Publishers Inc.

Cromer, R. F. 1974. The development of language and cognition: the cognition hypothesis. In B. Foss (Ed.) *New Perspectives in Child Development.* Harmondsworth: Penguin Books.

Crystal, D. 1987. *The Cambridge Encyclopaedia of Language.* Cambridge: Cambridge University Press.

Foss, B. (Ed.) 1974. *New Perspectives in Child Development.* Harmondsworth: Penguin Books.

Ferguson, C. and Slobin, D. 1973. *Studies of Child Language Development.* New York.

Ingram, D. 1989. *First Language Acquisition: Methods, Description and Explanation*. Cambridge University Press.

Lenneberg, E. H. 1967. Biological foundations of language. In E. H. Lenneberg (Ed.) *New Directions in the Study of Language.* Cambridge: Mass: MIT Press.

Slobin, D. 1973. Cognitive prerequisites for development of grammar. In C. Ferguson & D. Slobin. *Studies of Child Language Development*. New York, 175–208.

Snow, C. E. and Ferguson, C. A. (eds.) 1977. *Talking to Children: Language Input and Acquisition*. Cambridge University Press.

White, L. and Newson, M. 1989. *Universal Grammar and Second Language Acquisition*. Amsterdam/Philadelphia, PA: John Benjamins.

Chapter 3: Second Language Acquisition

The chapter attempts to provide insights on *how an L2 is acquired* by manipulating the following approaches of second language acquisition:

1. Behavioristic Approach
2. Cognitive/Psychological Approach
3. Creative Construction Approach
   a. The Acquisition-learning hypothesis
   b. The Monitor hypothesis
   c. The Natural-order hypothesis
   d. The Input hypothesis
   e. The Effective filter hypothesis
4. Sociological Approach

The following questions, among others, will be tackled here:

1) How important are imitation and practice for SLA?
2) To what extent can theories of acquiring a first language be applied to second/foreign language learning?

3.1 Introduction

The process of learning a second language (L2) takes place through different means. An L2 may be learned simultaneously or successively with the first language (L1). In the latter case, an L2 may be learned at various age stages (childhood, adolescence, or adulthood). It may also be learned in either an L1 or an L2 environment. In the former case, it is usually learned through instruction, while in the latter case, an L2 is usually learned through verbal contact with native speakers in a natural environment (see Figure 3.1).

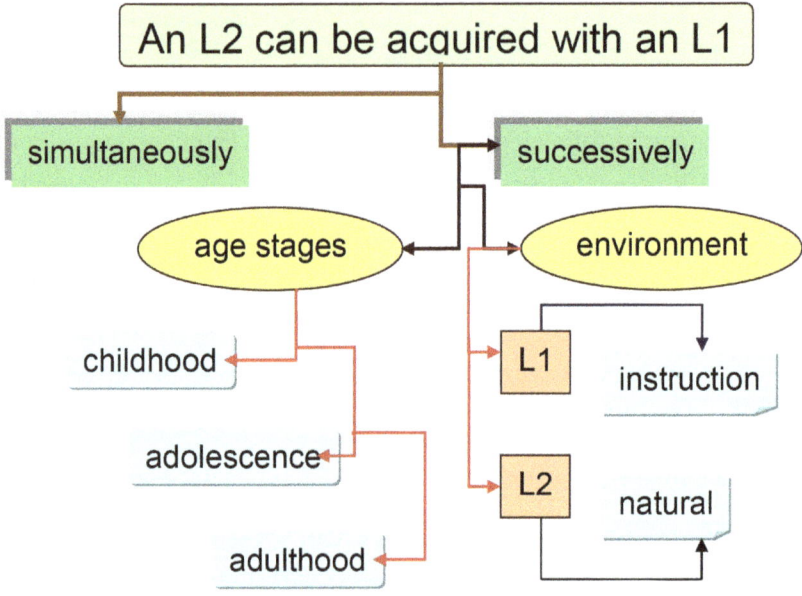

Figure 3.1: Ways of learning an L2.

The aforementioned distinction between L2 learning in an L1 environment (i.e. via instruction) and L2 learning in an L2 environment (i.e. through verbal contact with native speakers in a natural environment) encouraged some researchers such as (Krashen, 1981) to distinguish between *'acquisition'* and *'learning'*. The former *(acquisition)* refers to the subconscious process of 'picking up' a language through exposure (i.e. no formal classroom setting) and the latter *(learning)* to the conscious process of studying the language (i.e. in a formal classroom setting). According to this view, it is possible for learners to 'acquire' or to 'learn' rules independently and at separate times. Although such a distinction may have validity, particularly for teachers, it is problematic because of the difficulty of demonstrating whether the knowledge learners possess is of the 'acquired' or 'learned kind'.[6] In this book, the terms 'acquisition' and 'learning' will be used interchangeably.

Second language acquisition (SLA) is a complex process, involving many interrelated determinants: the learner, the environment, the effect of L1, etc. Many studies have been carried out to determine the characteristics of SLA and the effect of many factors on the process of SLA. A great deal of speculative thinking about SLA has also been published. Based on classroom observation, especially in listening to accents and noting errors of foreign learners of English, many teachers and researchers have produced a whole body of literature on what needs to be taught in L2 classes. Efforts have also been made to answer the following, as well as other questions: How do individuals acquire an L2? What are the different thoughts and premises that have been offered in order to explain the process of SLA? Why do learners vary in acquiring L2s?

This chapter discusses several theoretical assumptions that have been offered as answers to the previous and other questions. The actual output, or learners' performance, will be discussed in Chapter Four. Four main theoretical concepts and approaches will be considered in turn: the Behavioristic Approach, the Cognitive or Psychological Approach, the Creative Construction Approach, and the Sociological Approach.

3.2 Historical Perspective

The field of SLA investigates how people attain proficiency in a language which is not their mother tongue. Over the years, the study of SLA has been undertaken from a variety of different perspectives. In the 1950s and 1960s, the primary objective was pedagogic. Researchers were interested in trying to improve the way in which an L2 was taught. Hence, they were interested in discovering how those languages were

---

6   We will refer to this point again when discussing the Creative Construction Approach of second language acquisition in 3.5.1.

learned. From the 1970s onward, the focus shifted from the teacher to the learner (e.g. in 1973, Oller and Richards published their book entitled: *Focus on the Learner*).

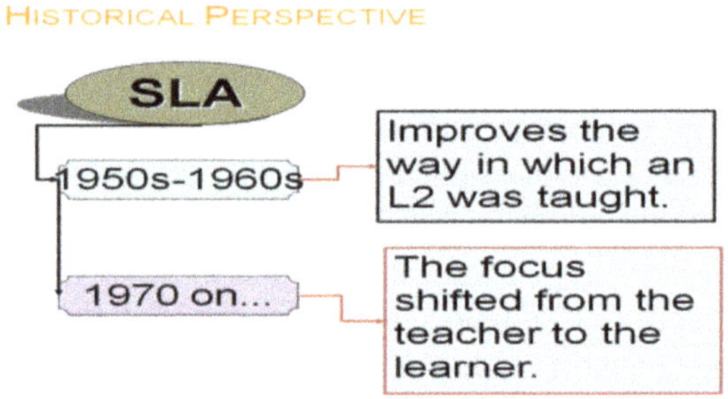

HISTORICAL PERSPECTIVE

- SLA
  - 1950s-1960s — Improves the way in which an L2 was taught.
  - 1970 on... — The focus shifted from the teacher to the learner.

Figure 3.2: The focus of SLA.

The reason for this shift was related to what was going on in linguistics, psychology, and L1 acquisition research. All three areas shifted the focus from external to internal factors which affected the processes in the 1960s. Linguistics became concerned with the mental grammar processes of the speaker, not just the description of the linguistic structures of a given language. This shift in emphasis was motivated by the need to understand the mechanisms underlying SLA (how an L2 is acquired?) and to ascertain whether the processes involved in the acquisition of L1 are similar to those involved in SLA.

Various answers and theoretical assumptions have been put forth to answer these and many other questions relating to various suppositions, such as behavioristic or empirical, cognitive or psychological and sociological, etc.

In the following sections, we will briefly discuss each of these approaches or assumptions.

3.3 Behavioristic Approach

Diller (1978) points out that authors, such as Bloomfield (1933), Skinner (1957), and many others (see also 2.2), held that SLA is a process of imitation and reinforcement. That is learners attempt to copy what they hear, and by regular practice they establish a set of acceptable habits in the new language.

Lado (1957) maintained that acquisition of L2 was essentially a task of overcoming the L1 habits and learning in their place the habits of the L2. Only those elements of the L2 which differed from L1 were considered important for learning. However, it was assumed that L2 learners transfer elements or skills[7] from their L1 to the L2. This transfer is considered to be *positive* when it facilitates learning or has a positive influence on the command of a skill or part of the L2 due to the similarity between the two languages. Transfer could also be considered *negative* when it impedes learning or has a negative influence on the command of a skill due to the difference between the two languages.[8] For an Arabic speaker learning English, an example of negative transfer would be the appearance of the resumptive pronoun in the relativized site:

* This is the house which I live in *it*.

The error in the above example *(it)* is a type of interference or negative transfer from Arabic (cf. Noor, 1996).

Another example of negative transfer from Arabic can be seen in the following example:

---

7   These include skills of learning or any part of the already acquired language, such as: vocabulary, structures, tenses, word order, etc.
8   Refer to Noor (1994) for a fuller discussion of the role of L1 in SLA.

a. An acceptable sentence in Arabic is: احمد رجل قوي /ʔaħmad radʒʊlʊn qawɪjʊn/⁹ 'Ahmad is a strong man.'
b. The English equivalent is: Ahmad (n.) is (fv.) a (art.) strong (adj.) man (n.)
c. Arab EFL learners may say: *Ahmad* (n.) *strong* (adj.) *man* (n.)

One can notice very clearly the absence of both the FV (function verb *is*) and the article (*a*) since both do not appear on the surface structure of the Arabic sentence (cf. Noor, 1996). Arab EFL learners may negatively transfer this construction from Arabic. The L1 habits hinder the learner in learning the forms of the L2.

An important part of this theory was 'contrastive analysis' (CA), the goal of which was to identify and catalogue the structural similarities and differences between languages. This was to help pinpoint areas of similarities and differences among the languages concerned. Areas of similarity, according to the CA hypothesis, are predictable and aid the acquisition process. Conversely, areas of difference are predictable and impede the acquisition process. This information was supposed to aid in planning the language-teaching materials which stressed the oral practice of the L2 sentence patterns. The main aim of behavioristic teaching is, thus, to form new, correct linguistic habits through intensive practice and in eliminating interference errors in the process of SLA.

3.3.1 *Critical Evaluation of the Behavioristic Approach*

Many researchers have criticized behaviorists' views. They are of the opinion that:

1- Imitation alone does not provide a means of identifying the task that learners face. The learning task is more complex than habit-formation. It is perhaps even more complex than any other learning task that most human beings undertake.

---

9   These phonetic transcriptions in Arabic, which are tabulated in the Appendix, are based on the IPA.

2- Transfer alone does not fulfill the function of explaining the learner's behavior in the L2. Many errors that are theoretically predicted by the differences between L1 and L2, in fact, do not occur in the language of learners, and conversely other errors that are committed by the learners seem unrelated to the L1. For example, L2 learners produce errors such as *seed* and *taked* (for the irregular Past-Tense forms) instead of *saw* and *took*.
3- L2 learners have intuitions that certain features of their L1 are less likely to be transferable than others. For example, most of the learners know intuitively that idiomatic or metaphorical expressions cannot simply be translated literally. For example, the (colloquial) Arabic expression (سقطت من عيني) /saqatˁta mɪn ʕaɪni:/ cannot be translated into *You fell from my eyes*. An Arabic learner knows intuitively that this translation would lead him to error.

All this suggests that the influence of the learner's L1 on learning an L2 is not simply a matter of habits. SLA is a much more elusive and complex process. As in L1 acquisition, the behavioristic account has proven to be at best an incomplete explanation of SLA (see 2.2).

3.4 Cognitive/Psychological Approach

The main alternative to the behavioristic approach can be the vital role of cognitive factors in SLA. Cognitive factors involve the mechanics of how an individual acquires something. From the cognitive perspective, SLA is viewed as the acquisition of a complex cognitive skill. This skill is composed of various sub-skills or aspects of performance (e.g., performance A (a pattern or expression) and performance B (tense, preposition, etc.) which must be practiced and integrated to achieve fluent performance. This requires the automatism of sub-skills, i.e. through experience and practice. L2 learners become able to use some of their knowledge so quickly and spontaneously that they are not even aware of doing it. This makes them focus on other aspects of the language (i.e. another performance) which gradually becomes automatic (see Figure 3.3).

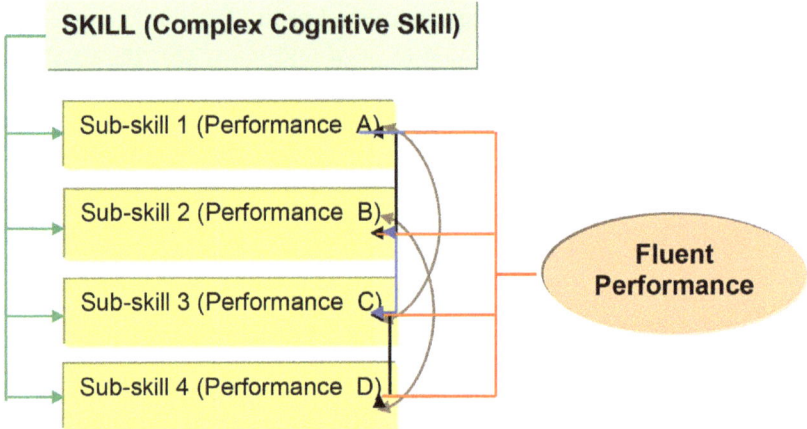

Figure 3.3: SLA according to the cognitive view.

Examples of part-skill (performance) practice are where an L2 learner may practice using a grammatical structure such as the negative, or express a communicative function like asking for permission. For instances of 'whole-task practice', an L2 learner may have to take part in a conversation or write a letter. This total skill (the whole skill) may be practiced, requiring the component parts to be integrated during performance.

Recently, cognitive psychologists have also investigated a phenomenon which is called *'restructuring'*. This refers to the observation that there is an interaction between the element the learner is learning and the knowledge he has already acquired (see Figure 3.4).

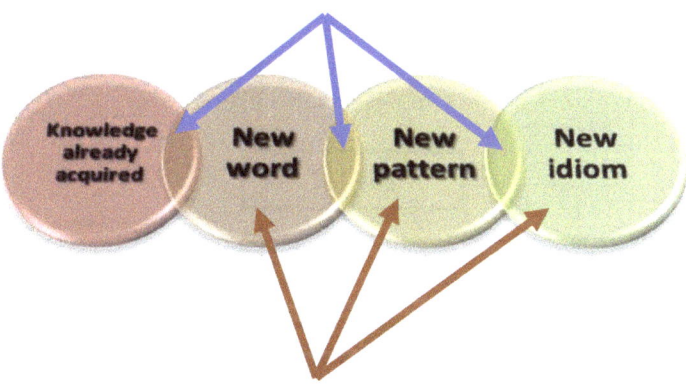

Figure 3.4: Restructuring.

With this interaction, the learner may restructure the system (language) he/she has or acquires. An L2 learner's performance improves and develops through constant reorganizing and restructuring of information contained in this system. This allows an L2 learner to simplify and unify linguistic information, and to gain increasing control of language performance.

3.5 Creative Construction Approach

Although Chomsky does not discuss the implications of his innatist's view (cf. 2.3) for SLA, others have proposed an approach which is, in some respect, similar to Chomsky's ideas on L1 acquisition. This approach is sometimes called the *Creative Construction Hypothesis*. In this hypothesis, a learner 'constructs' a series of internal representations of the L2 system. That is, the learner makes images of the elements (sounds and structures) of the L2 in his/her mind when he/she is *exposed* to the L2 in *communicative situations*. These internal representations occur as a result of natural processing strategies, such as generalization, transfer, etc. and exposure to the L2 in communicative surroundings. If the right kind of exposure takes place, the learner's internal representations develop gradually, in predictable stages, in the direction of the L2 system.

This hypothesis is similar to ones proposed for L1 acquisition (see 2.3). Figure 3.5 below represents this hypothesis.

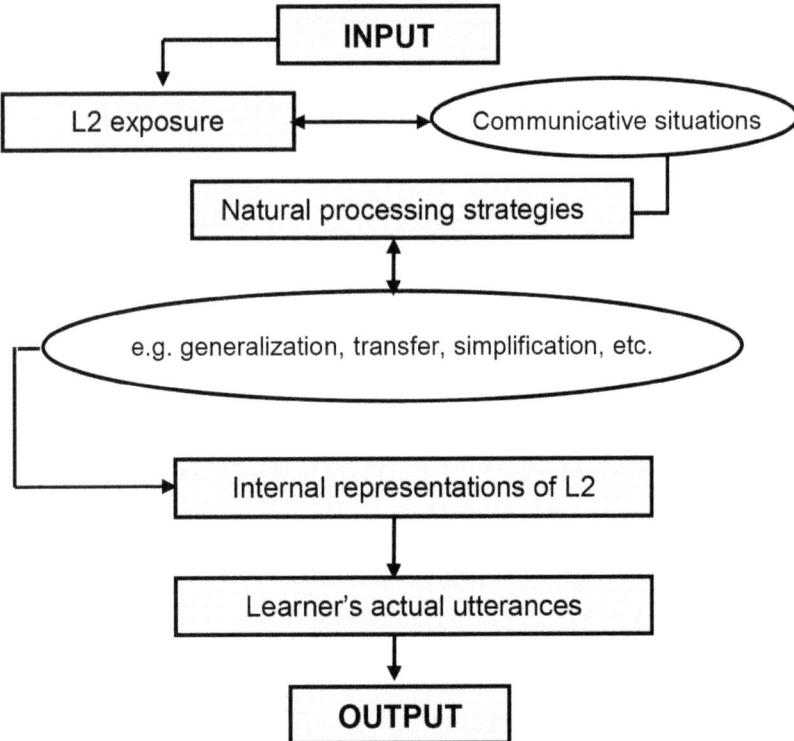

Figure 3.5: SLA as Creative Construction.

What is interesting in this hypothesis is its claim that internal processing strategies operate on input from the language environment and are not directly dependent on the learners' attempts themselves to produce the language. In other words, input which is available in the environment will make internal processing mechanisms (natural processing strategies) operate, but not the learner himself or his attempts to produce the language. That is, acquisition takes place internally as learners hear and read samples of the language that they understand. The speech and writing (i.e. the actual performance) which the learner eventually produces is seen as an outcome of the learning process rather than as the cause of learning, or even as a necessary step in learning. However, learners' utterances still play an important indirect role, since they enable learners to take part in communicative situations and thus gain more input. Figure 3.6 below represents the natural processing strategies with examples of the errors Arab learners may commit.

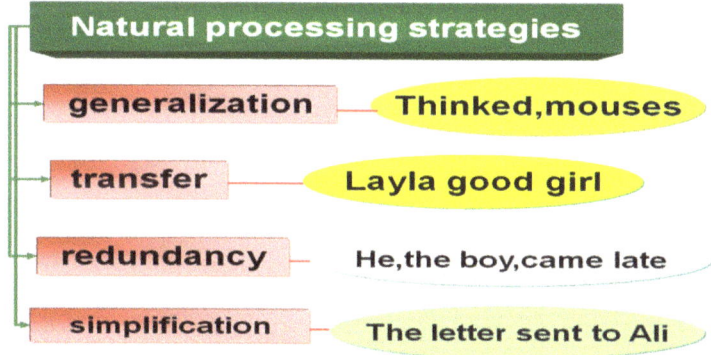

Figure 3.6: Natural Processing Strategies.

Evidence of Creative Construction

Most of the evidence of the Creative Construction Hypothesis has come from the analysis of learners' errors at various points in their SLA, and the order or sequence in which certain structures are acquired.

Krashen (1982) produced the creative construction hypothesis or theory. In a series of his works, Krashen has developed an overall theory of SLA. Five main hypotheses constitute his 'monitor model'. They are:

(1) the acquisition-learning hypothesis;
(2) the monitor hypothesis;
(3) the natural order hypothesis;
(4) the input hypothesis; and
(5) the affective filter hypothesis.

These hypotheses are as follows:

3.5.1 The Acquisition-learning Hypothesis

Krashen (1982) argues that language input provided by information 'intake'[10] is processed in a way which is different from input made available through explicit teaching of grammatical rules. He calls the first process *'acquisition'* and the second *'learning'*.

Acquisition is described by Krashen (1982:10) as:

> "[...] similar to the way children develop ability in their first language". It is a "[...] subconscious process; language acquirers are not usually aware of the fact that they are acquiring language, but are only aware of the fact that they are using the language for communication."

"[...] *learning is 'knowing the rules', having a conscious knowledge about grammar*" (Krashen and Terrel 1983:18). Acquisition is actually helpful for the L2 learner. Learning may be too rapid or difficult through explicit teaching. In performance, 'acquired' knowledge serves as the major source for initiating both the comprehension and production of utterances. It contains all information the learner has acquired or obtained of the L2 except the metalinguistic knowledge or the grammatical rules which explain how the language is structured. This knowledge

---

10   *Intake* or useful input is considered to be a rich environment where the learner is actively involved.

is available through learning and is used by the learner to control the language he or she produces, i.e. through the Monitor.

3.5.2 The Monitor Hypothesis

The Monitor is a device that learners use to edit their own language performance. The monitor utilizes 'learned' knowledge (or competence) by modifying utterances which are generated from the *'acquired'* knowledge (or competence). This can occur either before or after the utterance (see Figure 3.7).

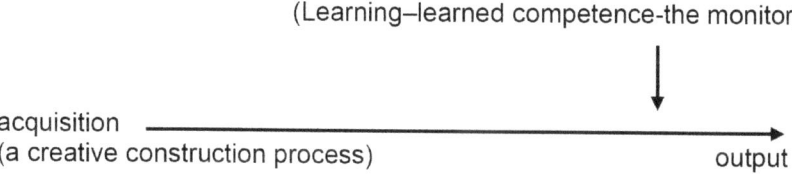

Figure 3.7: Krashen's monitor hypothesis. (from Johnson, 2001:92)

Krashen states that there are three conditions which have to be met for the Monitor to come into use:

1- the learner has some knowledge of the required grammatical rule;
2- sufficient time is required for editing;
3- the learner's attention is focused on the location and nature of the grammatical form.

Krashen (1982) argues that editing can also take place by using *'acquired'* competence. He refers to this process of acquisition as editing by 'feel' right or 'feel' wrong regarding errors.

3.5.3 The Natural-order Hypothesis

This hypothesis presumes that language learners acquire properties of an L2 in a predictable order, going through a series of common transitional stages in moving towards target/second language forms. However, when the L2 learner is engaged in tasks that require the use of metalinguistic knowledge,[11] a different order of acquisition will emerge. Studies of morpheme and conjunction acquisition are evidence of this hypothesis. These studies show that data collected under conditions that need communication, show a similar order of difficulty while tests focused on grammatical correctness led to a different order of acquisition.

3.5.4 The Input Hypothesis

What is Input?

Input is what the learner hears, reads, sees, or feels inside and outside the classroom. Input is the most important factor in SLA. It affects the progress of the learner in learning the L2.

If the learner has to make progress beyond a given stage of acquisition, he must be exposed to the most comprehensible input.

This comprehensible input has three characteristics:

(1) Comprehensive (i.e. covers the area to be presented);
(2) Adequate for the level of the learners, and
(3) Clear (in pronunciation) and correct (in grammar).

Krashen (1982) terms this process as i+1. Where the i stands for the current level of the second language learner and the 1 is the next structure for the acquirer to learn. This means that acquisition may take place as a result of the acquirer having understood input which contains linguistic items that are slightly beyond the learner's present linguistic competence. This can be presented diagrammatically in Figure 3.8 below.

---

[11] That is knowledge available through the explicit presentation of grammatical rules.

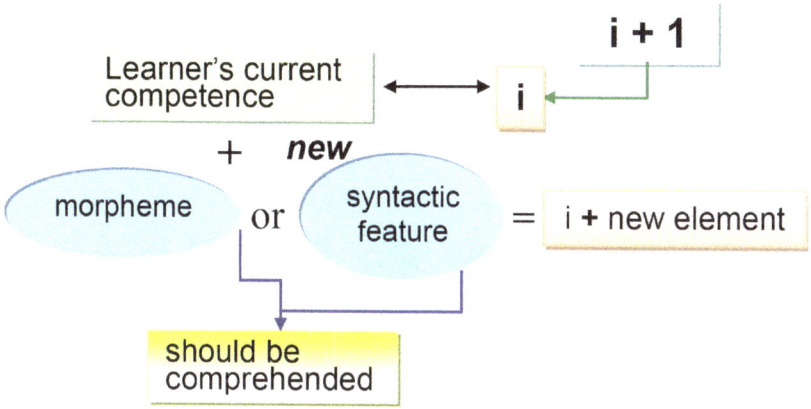

Figure 3.8: i+1 Hypothesis (Krashen, 1982).

The learner makes progress gradually until he acquires a mature-state of grammar, i.e. he will be able to speak an acceptable form of the language.

3.5.5 *The Affective-filter Hypothesis*

This approach deals with how affective non-linguistic factors relate to SLA.[12] An *'affective filter'* is an imaginary barrier which prevents learners from using input available in the environment. The term, 'affect' refers to mental faculties like *motives*, *needs*, *attitudes*, and *emotional stress*. When the feelings of the learner are 'positive', we might say that he is more open to input. His filter is clean, and language passes easily through it. A learner with 'negative' feelings, or who feels tense, anxious, bored or is unmotivated, will, on the other hand, be 'closed' to input (see Figure 3.9 below).

---

12 Refer to Chapter 5 for a fuller discussion of the non-linguistic factors which affect the learning process.

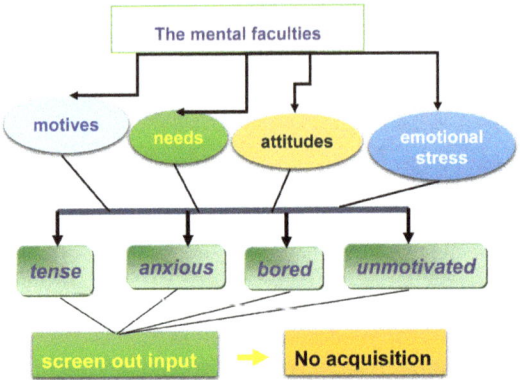

Figure 3.9: The affective filter.

The filter will be 'up' (or operating) when the learner is under stress, self-conscious, or in an unmotivated state. It will be 'down' (or not operating) when the learner is relaxed and motivated.

3.6 Sociological Approach

In the late 1970s and early 1980s, research began to give attention to the social context of adult SLA. This concept has generally come to be known as the *Sociological Approach or Acculturation*. Acculturation refers to the process of becoming adapted to the culture of the new or second language. This involves developing an understanding of the systems of thought, beliefs, and emotions of the new culture as well as its system of communication. Schumann (1978), for example, argues that the degree to which a learner acculturates or adapts to L2 native speakers will determine the extent of competence he acquires in the L2. According to this approach, acculturation is a function of the *social* and *psychological 'distance'* between the learner and native speakers of the L2.

If there is decrease in social distance then the learner's L2 will be very simple or will result in 'simplified' L2 grammar, sufficient only for communicative success, and lacking 'redundant' grammatically relevant properties. The lack in properties may include morphological inflections (-'s, -ing, etc.), function words such as determiners and auxiliaries, (his, that, is, was, etc.) subordinate clauses, (if he goes shopping, or while you're here, etc.) and so on. Development towards the L2 norm (i.e. what is acceptable by adult native learners) is dependent on the level of social distance between the learner and native speakers of the L2. If the social distance fails to decrease, the L2 learner's grammar will fossilize (i.e. learner's grammar becomes simplified). Individual learners will vary, too, depending on the extent to which they are willing or able to reduce the social distance.

Psychological distance is the result of various affective factors that concern the learner as an individual. These factors would include resolution of *language shock, culture shock* and *stress*, and *integrated* vs. *instrumental motivation*.[13]

Social and psychological distance influences SLA by determining the amount of contact with the L2 that the learner experiences, and also the degree to which he is exposed to available input. Thus, in *'bad'* learning situations the learner will receive very little L2 input. Also, when the psychological distance is above average, the learner will fail to convert available input into intake (i.e. he fails to get the best of this input and make it available when he retrieves acquired knowledge from his mind).

The acculturation model for SLA shows us why L2 learners often fail to achieve native-like competence due to social and/or psychological distance. However, this model fails to shed light on how L2 knowledge is internalized and used. Furthermore, the acculturation model fails to account for the role of interaction between the situation and the learner.

---

13 See Chapter 5.

3.7 Conclusion

What we have seen in this chapter attempts to answer, among others, one broad general question *"How is an L2 acquired"*? The answer was undertaken from different perspectives: psychological, sociological, linguistic, etc. We have seen the importance of *input* for stimulating and conditioning the language acquisition process. We have also noticed that the L2 learner is active not passive in the process of SLA. This learner is provided with an innate means to acquire the language, to use the language, and to communicate through the language. In addition to these, as a human being, the L2 learner will acquire the language through exposure (naturally or through instruction) and through interaction with the environment.

Acquiring an L2, as we have already seen, is not an easy phenomenon to explain. There are many interrelated factors affecting the acquisition process. In the following chapters, we will continue discussing these factors and see to what extent the L2 learner is active in the process of SLA by shedding some light on learners' performance, non-linguistic factors which affect the SLA process, and on the strategies that the L2 learner uses in dealing with the L2.

Study Questions

1. What are the different ways of learning an L2?
2. 'Before the late 1960s, SLA was almost exclusively related to teaching'. Discuss this notion and show how the emphasis was shifted to the L2 learner.
3. What does the learner do in learning another language according to the Behavioristic Approach?

4. Why is CA considered as one of the most important factors in the Behavioristic Approach of SLA?
5. What is the main aim of the behaviorists in L2 teaching?
6. What critical points face the Behavioristic Approach in SLA?
7. Explain with examples the terms 'positive transfer' and 'negative transfer'?
8. What is the main view of the Cognitive Approach?
9. How does 'the automatism of component sub-skills take place in SLA? Discuss this from the cognitive/psychological point of view.
10. What is *restructuring*?
11. According to the creative construction view of SLA, an L2 learner 'constructs' a series of internal representations of the L2 system', discuss how this operation takes place.
12. According to 'creative construction', are 'speech' and 'writing' an outcome of the learning process, or the cause of learning?
13. What is the difference between 'intake' and 'input'?
14. Do you agree that *acquisition* is a subconscious process? And why?
15. Explain how grammatical structures are 'acquired' in a predictable order?
16. What do we mean by 'the learner must be exposed to the most crucial comprehensible input in order to progress beyond a given stage of acquisition'?
17. What does 'the effective filter' in SLA mean?
18. How do social and psychological distances affect the process of SLA?

Projects

1. From the different thoughts and approaches of SLA you have studied here, give a comprehensive view of how a second language is acquired?

2. Four approaches of SLA have been presented in this chapter. Use the Internet to research this field and present one approach which is not mentioned here.
3. Can you think of a classroom situation in which the Monitor Hypothesis can be applied?
4. Do you agree with Krashen's (1982) classification of *acquisition* and *learning* mentioned here? Write an essay about this classification showing the different views of the linguists, including your opinion?

For Further Reading

General Discussion Of SLA

Ellis, R. 1986. *Understanding Second Language Acquisition*. Oxford University Press.

McLaughlin, B. 1987. *Theories of Second-Language Learning*. London: Edward Arnold.

Cook, V. 1993. *Linguistics and Second Language Acquisition*. London: The Macmillan Press.

Cook, V. 2001. *Second Language Learning and Language Teaching*. London: Edward Arnold.

Doughty, C. J. – Long, M.H. 2002. *The Handbook of Second Language Acquisition*. Oxford: Blackwell (Blackwell Handbooks in Linguistics).

Gass, S. & Selinker, L. 1994. *Second Language Acquisition an Introductory Course*. London: Erlbaum Associates, Publishers.

Huebner, T., and C. Ferguson (eds.) 1991. *Crosscurrents in Second Language Acquisition and Linguistic Theories*. Amsterdam: John Benjamins.

Larsen-Freeman, D. and M. Long 1991. *An Introduction to Second Language Acquisition Research*. New York: Longman.

Ortega, L. 2007. *Understanding Second Language Acquisition*. London: Hodder Arnold.
Ritchie, W. C., & Bhatia, T. K. (Eds.). 2009. *The New Handbook of Second Language Acquisition* (2nd Revised edition). Bingley: Emerald.
Saville-Troike, M. 2005. *Introducing Second Language Acquisition.* Cambridge: Cambridge University Press (Cambridge Introductions to Language and Linguistics).
Towell, R. & Hawkins, R. 1994. *Approaches to Second Language Acquisition*. Clevedon: Multilingual Matters.
VanPatten, B. – Williams, J. (Eds.) 2006. *Theories in Second Language Acquisition. An Introduction.* Mahwah, NJ: Lawrence Erlbaum Associates (Second Language Acquisition Research).

Behaviorism in SLA

Bloom, L.M. 1974. "Imitations in Language Development: If, When, and Why", *Cognitive Psychology*, pp. 380–420.
Brooks, Nelson 1960. *Language and Language Learning*. New York: Harcourt, Brace and World.
Lado, R. 1964. *Language Teaching: A Scientific Approach*. New York: McGraw-Hill.
Towell, R. & Hawkins, R. 1994. *Approaches to Second Language Acquisition*. Clevedon: Multilingual Matters.

Cognitive Theory

Christiansen, M.H. and Chater, N. (eds). 2001. *Connectionist Psycholinguistics*. Westport CO: Ablex.
Croft, W. and Cruise, A. 2004. *Cognitive Linguistics*. Cambridge: CUP.
McLaughlin, B. 1987. *Theories of Second-Language Learning*. London: Edward Arnold.

Pienemann, M. 1998. *Language Processing and Second Language Development: Processability theory.* Amsterdam: John Benjamins.

Tomlin, R. and M. A. Gernsbacher (eds.) 1994. Cognitive Foundations of Second Language Acquisition. *Studies in Second Language Acquisition*, Special Issue 16/2.

Creative Construction

Dulay, H., M. Burt and S. Krashen 1982. *Language Two.* Oxford: Oxford University Press.

Krashen, S. 1982. *Principles and Practice in Second Language Acquisition.* Oxford: Pergamon.

Acculturation Theory

Ellis, R. 1992. *Second Language Acquisition and Language Pedagogy.* Clevedon: Multilingual Matters.

Schumann, J. 1978. *The Pidginisation Process: A Model for Second Language Acquisition.* Rowley MA.: Newbury House.

Tarone, E. 1988. *Variation in Interlanguage.* London: Edward Arnold.

References

Bates, E., and Mac Whinney, B. 1981. Second language acquisition from a functionalist perspective. In H. Winitz (Ed.) *Native Language and Foreign Language Acquisition.* Annals of the NY Academy of Sciences, Vol. 379.

Bloomfield, L. 1933. *Language.* New York: Holt.

Brown, R. 1973. *A First Language: The Early Stages.* Cambridge. Mass.: Harvard University Press.

Burt, M. K. and H. C., Dulay 1980. On acquisition order. In S. W. Felix (Ed.) *Second Language Development: Trends and Issues.* Tubinger Beitrage zur Linguistik, 125. Tubingen: Gunter Narr, 265–327.

Chomsky, N. 1976. *Reflections on Language.* London: Temple Smith.

Chomsky, N. 1980. *Language and Problems of Knowledge: The Managua Lectures.* MIT Press.

Clark, H. and E., Clark 1978. Universals, relativity, and language processing. In Greenberg, J. (Ed.) *Method and Theory: Universals of Human Language.* Stanford University Press.

Cook, V. 1993. *Linguistics and Second Language Acquisition.* London: The Macmillan Press.

Cook, V. 2001. *Second Language Learning and Language Teaching.* London: Edward Arnold.

Diller, K. 1978. *The Language Teaching Controversy.* Rowley, Mass.: Newbury House.

Dulay, H. and M., Burt 1974. Natural sequences in child second language acquisition. *Language Learning* 24/1:37–53.

Eckman, F. 1977. Markedness and the contrastive analysis hypothesis. *Language Learning* 27/315–330.

Ellis, R. 1986. *Understanding Second Language Acquisition.* Oxford University Press.

Ellis, R. 1994. *The Study of Second Language Acquisition.* Oxford: Oxford University Press.

Gass, S. & Selinker, L. 1994. *Second Language Acquisition and Introductory Course.* London: Erlbaum Associates, Publishers.

Greenberg, J. 1968. *Language Universals. Theoretical Foundations: Current Trends in Linguistics*, vol. 3, Seboek (Ed.). The Hague: Mouton.

Hatch, E. M. 1983. *Psycholinguistics: a Second Language Perspective.* Rowley, Mass: Newbury House.

Johnson, K. 2001. *An Introduction to Foreign Language Learning and Teaching.* Longman: London.

Karmiloff-Smith, A. 1986. Stage/structure versus phase/process in modeling linguistic and cognitive development. In I. Levin (Ed.)

Stage and Structure: Reopening the debate. Norwood, NJ., Ablex. 164–90.

Kellerman, E. 1977. Towards a characterization of the strategy of transfer in second language learning. *Interlanguage Studies Bulletin* 2: 58–145.

Kilborn, K. and A. Cooreman 1987. Sentence interpretation strategies in adult Dutch-English bilinguals. *Applied Psycholinguistics*, 8: 415–31.

Krashen, S. 1977. Some issues relating to the monitor model. In Brown, H., Yorio, C., and Crymes, R. (eds.) *TESOL '77: Teaching and Learning English as a Second Language: Trends in Research and Practice.* (pp. 144–158), Washington: TESOL.

Krashen, S. 1981. *Second Language Acquisition and Second Language Learning.* Oxford: Pergamon Press.

Krashen, S. 1982. Accounting for child-adult differences in second language rate and attainment. In Krashen, S., Scarcella, R., and Long, M. (eds.) *Child-Adult Differences in Second Language Acquisition.* (pp. 202–226), Rowley, Mass.: Newbury House.

Krashen, S. and T. Terrel 1983. *The Natural Approach: Language Acquisition in the Classroom.* New York: Pergamon Press.

Lado, R. 1957. *Linguistics across Cultures.* Ann Arbor: The University of Michigan Press.

McLaughlin, B. 1987. *Theories of Second-Language Learning.* London: Edward Arnold.

Noor, H. H. 1994. Some implications on the role of mother tongue in second language acquisition. *Linguistica Communicatio* 6/1 & 2: 97–106.

Noor, H. H. 1996. English syntactic errors by Arabic Speaking Learners: reviewed. Paper presented at the 4th International Symposium on Languages and Linguistics, Jan. 8–10, 1996 (pp. 1441–65).

Oller, J., and Richards (eds.) 1973. *Focus on the Learner: Pragmatic perspectives for the language teacher.* Rowley, Mass.

Richards, J. C. 1971. A non-contrastive approach to error analysis. *ELT* 25/3: 204–219.

Rutherford, W. E. 1982. Markedness in second language acquisition. *Language Learning* 32/1:85–107.
Schachter, J. 1992. A new account of language transfer. In S. Gass and L. Selinker (eds.) *Language Transfer in Language Learning*. Amsterdam: John Benjamin.
Schumann, J. 1978. Social and psychological factors in second language acquisition. In J. Richards (Ed.) *Understanding Second and Foreign Language Learning: Issues and approaches*. Rowley, M. A.: Newbury House, 163–78.
Skinner, B. 1957. *Verbal Behavior*. New York: Appleton Century Crofts.
Towell, R. & Hawkins, R. 1994. *Approaches to Second Language Acquisition*. Clevedon: Multilingual Matters.
de Villiers, J. & P. de Villiers 1973. A cross-sectional study of the acquisition of grammatical morphemes in child speech. *Journal of Psycholinguistic Research* 2:267–78.

Chapter 4: Approaches To Learners' Performance

The chapter covers the following approaches regarding learners' performance:

1. Contrastive Analysis (CA)
2. Error Analysis (EA)
3. Interlanguage (IL)

Within these three approaches, the following questions will be tackled in general here:

(1) What are the errors committed especially by Arab EFL/ESL learners and what are their characteristics?
(2) What are the causes of these errors?
(3) What is the role of these errors in learning and teaching an L2?

4.1 Introduction

Learners' performance is the actual utterances that the learner produces. It contains both acceptable (i.e. correct) and unacceptable utterances (i.e. errors). Errors are considered important determinants of the SLA process.

In this chapter, three approaches to learners' performance (i.e. linguistic behaviour) will be discussed: Contrastive Analysis (CA), Error Analysis (EA) and Interlanguage (IL).

4.2 Contrastive Analysis (CA)

CA is a term introduced by behaviourists in order to explain how L1 habits interfere with or affect the L2 learning process (see 3.2). The *goal of CA* was to identify and catalogue the structural similarities and differences between languages. Similar structures or patterns (i.e. rules or concepts) between L1 and L2 are predicted to aid the L2 acquisition process, while different ones are predicted to impede such process. The similar patterns are easier to learn and are grasped more effortlessly because they are ingrained in the learner's behaviour. The dissimilar patterns are more difficult to learn because the learner needs to activate new efforts to form new ones in his behaviour. The habits which were transferred from the L1 to the L2 may constitute either facilitation or inhibition in learning the L2. This thinking led researchers in the 1960s to carry out large-scale projects of contrastive analysis between English and some European languages by the Center of Applied Linguistics in Washington, D. C. Thus, contrastive analysis (or linguistics) became one of the most flourishing areas of linguistic research in the late 1960s.

4.2.1 The Rationale of CA

The rationale for undertaking CA in L2 learning is derived mainly from the following two factors (Sridhar 1980:95–96):

1. *Practical experience of L2 teachers.*
   Through teaching L2s, teachers became aware of a substantial number of errors made by their students, which can be attributed to their L1s. For instance, Arab learners of English substitute /p/ with /b/ because /p/ does not occur in Arabic as a separate phoneme. It occurs in few cases as an allophone of /b/ as in the word /ḥaps/ 'prison' or 'holding or keeping back'.
2. *The theory of transfer.*
   The transfer in learning a task of an L2 is either facilitated or impeded by the learning of a previous task of an L1. This depends mainly on the similarity or difference between the tasks, as already explained by positive and negative transfers, which are derived from behaviouristic psychology (see 3.2). Figure 4.1 below is designed for an easy explanation of transfer.

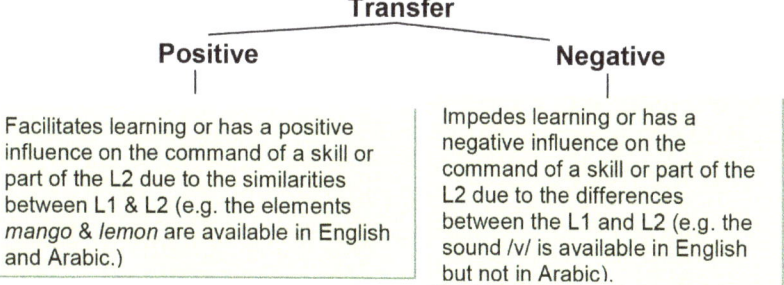

Figure 4.1: Types of Transfer.

L1 transfer in its negative aspect is very clear in pronunciation; this confirms what is called in the literature of applied linguistics, a foreign accent. The foreign accent is clearly recognized by linguists and also by native speakers of the L2. American native speakers, for example, can realize the distinctive accent of Arabs, Chinese, Japanese, Indians, and others when they speak English as an L2. L1 transfer is also involved in other linguistic levels. Gass (1979:328) clarifies this notion in her definition of transfer, "that patterns of the native language (of all levels of linguistic structure), including both forms and functions of elements, are superimposed on the patterns learned in a second language." For instance, Arab learners of English do not add the inflectional morpheme '-s' to the Present Tense of the verb when the subject is a third person singular (e.g., *he/she/it "come" instead of he/she/it "comes"), and they use the Past Simple Tense of the verb more than the Present Perfect Tense (e.g. * 'Look what you did!' and * 'Did you see Ahmed today?' instead of 'Look what you have done!' and 'Have you seen Ahmad today?'). The first error is due to the fact that there is an absence of the third person Present Tense morpheme in Arabic and it is not psychologically (i.e. cognitively) productive for adult native-Arabic speakers (Al-Qadi 1997:12). The second error is attributable to the fact that there is no well-defined counterpart in Arabic to cover all the meanings of the Present Perfect Tense in English (Kharma and Hajjaj 1989:159–160). Schachter (1974) found that Arab and Persian students locate relative clauses in English after the head noun since this is the case in their L1s (e.g. *This is the person whom I met yesterday.* مس أ قابلته الذي الشخص هذا ha:ða aʃʃaχasˤ allaði qa:bltuhu ʔams/ and *The boy who left is British* /الولد الذي غادر بريطاني/ alwaladu alði ʁa:dara breɪtˤa:ni:/). In contrast, Chinese and Japanese students generally avoid using relative clauses since they occupy prenominal positions in their L1.

4.2.2 Factors of Negative Transfer

There are a number of factors responsible for negative transfer in the learner's performance (Van Els et al 1984:59–60):

1. *Limited quantity of L2 input*: negative transfer is likely to occur when L2 is learned in an L1 environment (e.g. learning English in the Arab world).

2. *Age*: negative transfer seems to appear more in adults' performance rather than in children's performance particularly in the first stages of an L2 learning process.
3. *Linguistic distance between L2 and L1*: negative transfer increases proportionally to the linguistic differences between the L2 and the learner's L1, as between English which is an Indo-European language and Arabic which is a Semitic language.
4. *Focus*: negative transfer is likely to occur if the learner's focus is only on correct grammatical forms rather than on successful communication.

4.2.3 CA Assumptions

Lee (1968:186) stated four assumptions for CA in the following manner:

1. The prime, or even the sole, cause of difficulty and error in L2 learning is interference coming from the learners' L1. In other words, L2 difficulties are chiefly, or wholly, due to the differences between the two contrasted languages.
2. The greater these differences are, the more acute the learning difficulties will be.
3. The results of a comparison between the two languages are needed to *predict* the difficulties and errors which may occur in learning the L2.
4. What there is to teach can best be found by comparing the two languages and then subtracting what is common to them (i.e. similarities), so that what the student has to learn equals the sum of the differences established by the CA.

4.2.4 CA Hierarchy of Difficulty

The linguists of the 1960s recognized different kinds of contrast between languages and attributed to them different degrees of difficulty.

Stockwell et al. (1965:282–291) established a hierarchy of difficulty that is also a hierarchy of learning an L2. This hierarchy of difficulty, from the greatest to the least, is as follows, with examples for Arab learners of English:

1. *Split*: L1 has one form, whereas the L2 has two or more (Arabic has one bilabial stop /b/, whereas English has two bilabial stops /p/ and /b/).
2. *New category*: It exists in the L2 but not in the L1 (Arabic does not have forms for indefiniteness but English has 'a' and 'an').
3. *Absent category*: It exists in the L1 but is absent in the L2. This happens when an English speaker learns the Arabic indefiniteness. It also occurs since English nouns normally have natural gender, whereas Arabic nouns have grammatical gender. Natural gender means that animate nouns are either masculine (male) or feminine (female) according to the sex of the referent noun.[14] Grammatical gender means that nouns are either masculine (e.g. /walad/ ولد 'boy'), feminine (e.g. /bınt/ بنت 'girl') or common (both masculine and feminine (e.g /tˤari:q/ طريق 'way'). This common gender is absent in English.
4. *Coalesced forms*: The L1 has two forms or more, whereas the L2 has one (Arabic has several negators, /la:/, /ma:/, /lajsa/, /lam/, /lan/ لا، ما، ليس، لم، لن whereas English has mainly one, 'not').
5. *Complete correspondence*: A form in an L1 is the same or roughly the same as a form in an L2. No difficulty arises with such correspondence (The Simple Past Tense is available in English and Arabic).

The heirarchy shows that difficulties will be the greatest when there is a split, and the least in the case of coalesced forms. It is noticed that the split is the opposite of coalesced forms and a new category is the inverse of an absent category.

---

14 However, inanimate nouns are neuter in gender. Few English animate nouns are morphologically or lexically marked for gender. Some morphologically marked nouns are actor/actress, host/hostess and hero/heroine. Some lexically marked nouns are boy/girl and man/woman.

4.2.5 CA Methodology

Accurate and explicit descriptions of languages under comparison are a prerequisite for any CA. These descriptions should already be made, or can be made by a competent researcher. With the availability of such descriptions, the CA will be undertaken by using the following technique (see Sridhar 1980:96–99):

1. Select tasks to be compared. Note that one cannot select prepositions in English and compare them with articles in Arabic.
2. The tasks selected should be compatible from a theoretical point of view. Compatibility is on the deep structure, since constructions have identical deep structures, even if they are markedly different on the surface structure. Chomsky presented the two sentences:

> John is easy to please.
> John is eager to please.

to indicate that their surface structures are the same but their deep structures (i.e. meanings) are completely different. The meaning in the first sentence is that it is easy to please John by other people, whereas the meaning in the second is that it is John himself who would like to please other people.
3. The tasks selected in the contrasted languages should be described in the same way, i.e. using the same model of description, such as traditional, structural, generative, etc.
4. Find out points of similarity and contrast (i.e. predictions of possible positive and negative transfers).
5. Develop teaching material on the possible positive and negative transfers.

However, new supporters of CA go beyond the five steps above of CA undertaking by using the following three ones:

1. Build hypotheses on the possible positive and negative transfers and empirically test these hypotheses, i.e. checking the predictions

against data from L2 learners' performance through the way of oral, written tests, interviews or questionnaires.
2. Analyze the data and then accept or reject the hypotheses.
3. Build teaching material on the obtained results, especially if other researchers support these results.

4.2.6 CA Technique: An Example

The CA technique is exemplified in Yes/No questions in English and Arabic by using the traditional model of structure:

1. Arabic description:
   Statement: هذه طالبة مجدة. /ha:ðɪhɪ tˤa:lɪbatʊn mʊdʒɪddah/
   Yes/No questions: هل هذه طالبة مجدة؟ - أ هذه طالبة مجدة؟ /hal ha:ðɪhɪ tˤa:lɪbatʊn mʊdʒɪddah/ /ʔha:ðɪhɪ tˤa:lɪbatʊn mʊdʒɪddah/
   The statement is only introduced by *a question word* الهمزة أو هل (/ʔalhamzah/or /hal/) to form the question.
2. English description:
   A: Statement: They are good boys.
   Yes/No question: *Are they good boys?*
   Only the verb *to be (are)* is moved to the front to form the question.
   B: Statement: She came late.
   Yes/No question: *Did she come late?*
   • The statement is introduced with the function verb (FV) *do* with its appropriate form to form the question.
   • The main verb (MV) is brought back to its infinitive form.
3. Contrast
   The contrast leads to the followig *differences*
   In A:
   1. In Arabic, a question word is only fixed at the beginning of the sentence.
   2. In English, the FV is moved to the front of the sentence.
   In B:
   1. In Arabic, no FV like English *do* is used.

2. In English, the FV *do* is used with its appropriate form at the beginning of the sentence and the MV is used with its infinitive form.
4. Hypotheses

   In A: It can be predicted that Arab learners of English will commit errors in not moving the FV to the front.

   In B: It can be predicted that Arab learnes of English will commit errors in not fixing the FV *do* at the front, putting it in its appropriate form and returning the MV to its infinitive form.

These predictions are useful in building teaching material for Yes/No questons in English for Arab learners, especially after emprical testing.

4.2.7 CA and L2 Teaching

On the basis of the CA assumptions discussed above (cf. 4.2.3), a number of claims have been made for L2 teaching:

1. The most effective teaching material to be learned by L2 learners are those that are based upon a CA between a learner's L1 and an L2. This includes the selection of teaching items, the degree of emphasis, different kinds of practice drills, etc.
2. Criteria for selecting testing items can ideally be done on the basis of CA.
3. The importance of CA in choosing teaching material is generally evidenced as a method of preventing L1 transfer, remedying errors, and exploiting similarities between languages.
4. CA can be helpful in drawing up a curriculum.
5. CA is very useful in a homogeneous classroom (e.g. teaching English to Arab learners only) more than in a heterogeneous classroom (e.g. teaching English to Arabs, Chinese, Japanese, etc.). In the homogeneous classroom, Arab learners have almost the same ease and difficulty since they all have a similar background which is Arabic as their native language. This means that significant results for L2 learners could be achieved, as well as facilitating instruction for L2 teachers.

4.2.8 CA Critics

CA is mainly criticized for:

1. Being based on the *notion of 'habit-formation'*, which neglects the role of the mind in the SLA process.
2. *Adequate knowledge of languages to be contrasted* may not be possessed by some researchers. Some researchers may well know the L1 but not the L2 or vice versa. This deficiency on the part of researchers may produce imperfect similarities and differences between the contrasted languages.
3. *Overprediction of errors*: A number of predictions about difficulties in L2 learning, which are based on CA, were not confirmed by the actual performance of L2 learners, whether in speech or writing. The English affricate sound /tʃ/, for example, is predicted to be difficult for Arab learners since it does not exist in Arabic, but from the authors' experience with Saudi Arabian learners of English, it is not completely so.
4. *Underprediction of errors*: Certain errors cannot be discovered and justified on the basis of CA, such as * *goed*, * *comed* and **hurted*. These errors are not only committed by some learners of English as an L2, but also by children of English as an L1. These errors are simplifications as a result of an overgeneralization of a regular English pattern which is the Past Simple Tense in English.
5. The contrast between an L2 and an L1 alone does not tell much about *how a learner goes about the learning process* of a task.

4.2.9 CA Defense

1. Markham (1985:26) blamed those who rejected CA because they do not favour *the notion of 'habit-formation'* of behaviouristic psychology. CA is not necessarily connected with 'habit-formation', but it is based on the transfer theory as being an integral factor in the L2 learning process. In other words, CA is actually

indispensable in explaining L1 transfer into L2 learning. George (1972) estimated that approximately one-third of learners' errors can be traced to L1 transfer.
2. At present, different aspects of most known languages are written in English. This may reduce the criticism against researchers who do not have *adequate knowledge of the languages to be contrasted*, since through the help of the English language, languages may be compared.
3. *Overprediction* was defended by Schachter (1974:213) as it may be "due to poor analysis or poor predictions about what is difficult and what is not." She also added that it could be due to avoidance. "If a student finds a particular construction in the target language (i.e. an L2) difficult to comprehend, it is very likely that he will try to avoid producing it." Blum and Levenston (1978:401) indicated where language learners at advanced stages use avoidance:

"The motivation for avoidance at this stage can be morphological (preferring a regular verb to an irregular one), phonological (preferring the word that's easier to pronounce), graphological (preferring the writing of the word one knows how to spell) or void (preferring a word that has a clear translation-equivalent in the mother tongue to one that does not)."

These cases of avoidance can be exemplified in order as:

learn/learned	teach/taught
meet /miːt/	coward /kaʊəd/
hand	tongue
date (of the date-palm)	snow

Kleinmann (1977) and Schachter (1979) argued that CA should not be abandoned as a diagnostic tool for L2 learning problems because of its ability to account for at least some avoidance.
4. For *underprediction*, CA is not the only substantial approach for L2 learning and teaching. Tran-Thi-Chau (1975:135) argued that it is sufficient for CA to deal with no more than 50% of the learner's errors. Sridhar (1980:100), moreover, skillfully supported this idea by saying that "the proponents of [...] CA are the first to concede that CA does not account for all errors; they never claimed that it

did." In other words, CA is not the remedy which can be used by the L2 teachers, but it can be a very useful approach for them and can assist them in their duties.
5. CA is not the only approach criticized about *how a learner goes about the learning process of a task*. Such a process is far from reach.

4.3 Error Analysis (EA)

Learning an L2 in the late 1960s was almost exclusively related to teaching. Learners' performance or linguistic behaviour, particularly deviaitions or errors, was considered to be something trivial. The assumption was that the L2 learner would learn what he was taught and would learn nothing that he was not taught. Discussions were flourishing about teaching methods and also about CA. If errors occurred, in spite of teaching, these errors were invariably attributed to L1 transfer; hence, the role of CA became very significant. During the fifties and the sixties, CA enjoyed respectability and enthusiasm. At the end of the 1960s, researchers began to realize that not all errors in L2 learning could be explained on the basis of linguistic differences between L1 and L2. Moreover, CA was seen to concentrate on the L2 teacher rather on the L2 learner. This led to a shift from teaching to learning and a concentration on error (i.e. inappropriate form) that learners regularly produce in the process of learning an L2. This approach focuses on the learner, and it is called error analysis (EA). *EA* is a technique which aims to describe and explain the systematic nature of deviations or errors generated in the learner's language.

4.3.1 The Importance of EA

The importance of the EA technique is listed in the following points:

1. It may play a role in understanding the processes that underlie L2 learning.
2. It figures out statistically the troublesome linguistic areas on errors that L2 learners encounter in learning.
3. Errors provide valuable feedback to both teachers and learners regarding learner's strategies and progress.

4.3.2 EA and CA Differences

EA is different from CA in:

1. EA is not restricted to errors caused by negative transfer from the L1; it brings to light many errors frequently committed by learners, such as 'overgeneralization errors'. For example, foreign English language learners overgeneralize the rule of the plural morpheme '-s' to *childs, instead of the correct form 'children'.
2. EA, unlike CA, provides data on real problems and this may lead to correct solutions in L2 teaching.
3. EA is not confronted with problems such as accurate and explicit descriptions of languages, compatibility, adequate knowledge of the contrasted languages, etc., that CA may face.

4.3.3 EA Methodology

EA is undertaken by using the following technique (Sridhar 1980:103):

1. Collection of errors: by using free compositions of learners around a theme or from their answers to examinations in English, or certain designed tests.

2. Identification of errors: by telling what kind of deviation from the L2 norm is and what a language variety (e.g. British or American English) and form (i.e. spoken or written) are.
3. Classification of error types (see figure 4.2 for error classification with examples for Arab EFL students).
4. Statement of relative frequency of error types.
5. Identification of the areas of difficulty in the L2.
6. Determination of the source of errors such as L1 transfer, overgeneralization, inconsistencies in the spelling system of the L2, etc.
7. Determination of the seriousness of the error in terms of communication and the L2 itself.
8. Remedy by the teacher in the classroom by designing special drills, lessons, activities, exercises, etc.

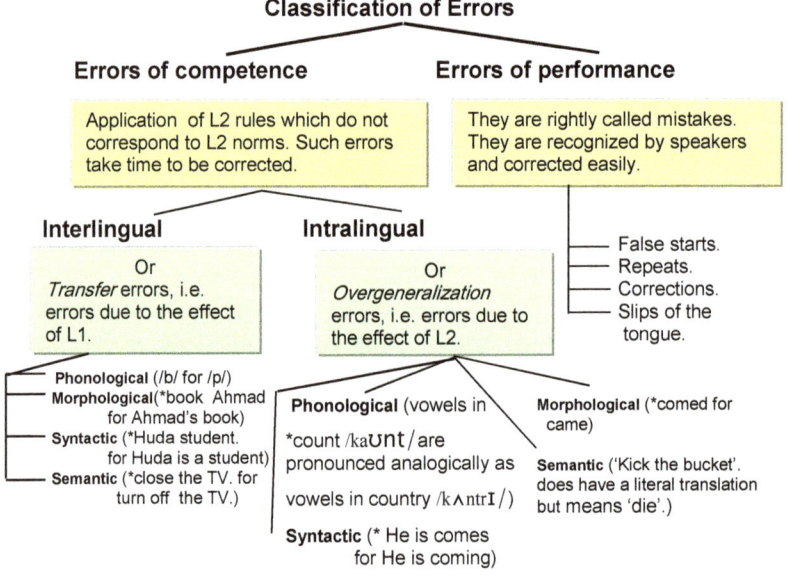

Figure 4.2: Classification of Errors.

4.3.4 EA Critics

EA is mainly criticized for:

1. *Classification of errors*: Errors may be wrongly classified between language tasks. The same error may be classified as interlingual and intralingual, e.g *he intelligent. This error was often committed by both English children and Arab learners. The error source for Arab learners may be due to the fact that the Arabic language has verbless sentences at the surface structure.
2. *Stresses only what the learner cannot do at a given point in time*. This was discovered by a cross-sectional study, which investigated an aspect at a single point in time for a number of learners with different degrees of proficiency. This means that EA does not provide any insight into the progression of the L2 learning process that can be achieved through longitudinal studies. Such studies are to investigate an aspect over a long period of time.
3. *Difficulty of error identification*: Errors are contrasted with L2 norms and these norms depend on, among other things, spoken or written language, formal or informal contexts, monitored or unmonitored speech, and symmetrical or asymmetrical relations between a researcher and learners.
4. *Avoidance strategy*: Learners simply avoid certain linguistic structures in which they would be likely to commit errors. It is possible that learners utilize such a strategy because of the differences between L2 and L1.

4.4 Interlanguage (IL)

Applied linguists had a new look at learners' performance because of the following:

1. A shift in psychology from behaviouristic to cognitive theories.
2. Dissatisfaction with L1 transfer as the main objective of CA.
3. Finding actual errors at a given point in time by the EA approach.

This new approach is no longer based on deviation (i.e. error) from the L2 norm at a given point in time, but on the processes of L2 development (i.e. at all levels: phonological, morphological, syntactic and semantic) as a whole in different stages. (see Figure 4.3). Attention is paid to the developmental processes and how one could account for both systematicity and variability in the learner's language.

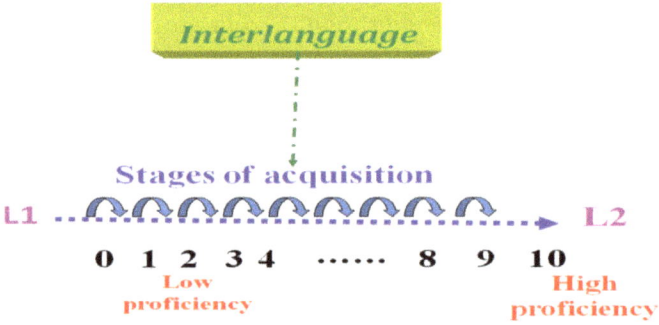

Figure 4.3: Interlanguage.

The hypothesis of this new approach was developed from the observation that adult learners of an L2 produce speech which is different from the acceptable L2 forms, and it is not always attributed to L1 transfer. The claim does not deny the possibility of both positive and negative transfers. This new approach is seen as a separate linguistic system from the L1 and the L2. This linguistic system has been called different terms, such as 'approximative systems' (Nemser 1971), 'interlanguage'

(Selinker 1969) and 'transitional competence' (Corder 1967). The most popular term is 'interlanguage' (IL) which represents the intermediate status of the learner's system between his L1 and the L2.

4.4.1 IL Assumptions

The main IL assumptions are the following:

1. *Learners internally construct a linguistic system*, which is different from both the learner's L1 and the L2, but it is based on L2 input that they receive.
2. *At successive stages of learning*, learners rely on their own linguistic system for reconstructing and approximating a certain variety of L2 that rarely becomes identical to the L2 norm.

4.4.2 Cognitive Processes of IL

Selinker (1972) argued that IL is the product of five central cognitive processes involved in L2 learning:

1. *L1 transfer.*
2. *Transfer of training*, which comes from learners' teachers.
3. *Strategies of L2 learning*, which are approaches by learners to the elements to be learned.
4. *Strategies of L2 communication*, which are ways of communicating with the native speakers of the L2.
5. *Overgeneralization of L2 rules*, which is a process by which a learner extends the L2 rule beyond its acceptable use.

On the basis of these cognitive processes, IL rules or descriptions should be made in consideration of the individual variations of learners and psychological (i.e. in 1, 3 and 5) and social (i.e. in 2 and 4) processes in L2 learning and teaching.

4.4.3 IL and Similarities with Natural Languages

IL as a linguistic system has the following similarities with natural languages:

1. *IL is assumed to be systematic* (i.e. governed by rules 'rule-governed behaviour'), such as SVO in English, but not VSO as in Arabic, and Adj. + N in English, but not N + Adj. as in Arabic, etc.
2. *IL shows evidence of internal consistency* since it is a linguistic system in its own right with forms that neither belong to the native langauge nor the target langague.
3. *IL obeys universal constraints at all levels* (i.e. phonological, morphological, syntactic and semantic) which occur in all natural languages, such as the following: languages have singulars and plurals; when there is a dual, there should be a plural; sentences have both deep structures and surface structures with which the surface structure is derived by one or more than one transformation, etc.

4.4.4 IL and Natural Differences in Languages

The IL rules or descriptions may differ considerably from natural language rules in the following:

1. *Reduced systems*: ILs are reduced systems with regard to the number and complexity of different rules (i.e. rules of phonology, morphology, lexis, syntax, semantics, and pragmatics).
2. *Permeability*: IL rules are typically permeable in the sense that they are by nature incomplete and in a state of flux because learners may use a rule or a form from their L1 and they may distort or overgeneralize a rule from the L2 in an attempt to convey the intended meaning. On the basis of this view, the rules of natural languages are relatively *stable.*
3. *Fossilization*: The cognitive representation is fixed in which aspects of pronunciation, vocabulary usage, and grammatical rules become a permanent part of the way a learner speaks or writes the L2, no

matter if there is more exposure to the L2 or new teaching. Selinker and Lamendella (1978) stated the possible causes for fossilization:
1. *Low motivation* of L2 learning for psychological and social reasons.
2. *Age* with which old learners usually retain a recognizable foreign accent.
3. *Limited range of L2 input* with respect to its quality and quantity.

4.4.5 IL Methodology

Selinker (1972:214) identified the essential components for IL analysis in:

1. L1 utterances produced by the learner.
2. IL utterances produced by the learner (the learner's version of L2).
3. L2 utterances used by its native speakers.
   In this way, IL methodology incorporates the assumptions of CA and EA. CA contrasts the learner's L1 and the L2, whereas EA basically contrasts the learner's performance and the L2.

4.4.6 IL and L2 Teaching

On the basis of the above IL assumptions, a number of claims have been made in L2 teaching:

1. The teacher of an L2 can get a clearer picture of the learner's transitional competence, which are not only the errors that are made at a particular time, as in the case of the EA approach.
2. Plans for teaching are done for the different stages of development.
3. Psychological and linguistic processes of L2 learning may be inferred from the descriptions of the learner's IL, as these descriptions develop and change through various attempts of learning the L2.

4. Our realistic aim in L2 teaching and learning is not to achieve native-speaker competence, but something near it.

4.4.7 IL Critics

IL's are mainly criticized for:

1. No concrete assertions are made in the IL literature on how to describe the changing linguistic systems in IL.
2. A large body of data is needed to ascertain a linguistic rule in the learner's IL. This is only achieved through longitudinal studies, which take a long period of time (i.e. years) in order to follow the development of a language phenomenon.
3. Observation of the most truly systematic form of a learner's IL is not an easy process since it needs a number of considerations related to the social status of the learners and the researcher, the topic of discourse, the spoken or written language, a naturalistic or experimental task, the physical surroundings (e.g. classroom, home, office, etc.), and monitored or unmonitored speech.

4.5 Conclusion

Learners' performance as the cornerstone of SLA was generally investigated within three approaches: CA, EA and IL. Errors as important factors of the SLA processes were also analysed with the help of the three approaches by showing their charateristics, causes and their role in L2 learning and teaching. This brief discussion was exemplified with reference to Arab learners of English as a FL/SL.

Study Questions

1. What is meant by 'the learners' performance'?
2. What was the goal of CA?
3. Why are similar patterns easier to learn and dissimilar ones more difficult to learn?
4. State and explain the two assumptions for undertaking CA in L2 learning.
5. What are the effects of positive and negative transfers? Illustrate your answer with examples.
6. What does it mean that 'learning is a matter of habit-formation'?
7. Exemplify 'the foreign accent'.
8. Define transfer and give examples for Arab learners of English.
9. State and explain the factors which are responsible for negative transfer in a learner's performance.
10. Explain the four assumptions of CA.
11. State and explain the five degrees of the hierarchy of difficulty in learning an L2 and provide examples for each one of them in the case of Arab learners learning English.
12. What are the five steps of conducting a CA and what are the prerequisites of performing a CA?
13. What do new supporters of CA do in undertaking a CA?
14. Explain the five claims in L2 teaching as a result of CA.
15. Explain the five points of CA critics.
16. Do you agree with the point that CA does not reveal anything about the learning process and why?
17. Defend the following points of CA critics: the notion of 'habit-formation', adequate knowledge by researchers of the languages to be contrasted, and overprediction and underprediction.
18. Where do advanced learners use avoidance? Illustrate your answer with examples.
19. Explain the shift from teaching/teacher to learning/learner in which it is the shift from CA to EA.
20. Put the importance of EA into points.

21. What is the difference between CA and EA?
22. Classify learners' errors and illustrate your answer at least with one example.
23. What are the eight steps of making an EA?
24. Explain the four points of EA critics.
25. What are the three reasons for the rise of IL.
26. What does IL depend on?
27. Where does the IL hypothesis develop from?
28. Explain the two assumptions of IL.
29. What are the five cognitive processes in L2 learning which led to IL? Which ones are related to psychological processes and which are related to social processes?
30. What are the similarities between IL and natural languages?
31. What are the differences between IL and natural languages?
32. What is meant by 'permeability' and 'fossilization'?
33. What are the three causes of fossilization?
34. What are the three essential components of IL analysis?
35. In what ways does IL incorporate CA and EA?
36. Explain the four claims of L2 teaching with reference to IL.
37. On what points is IL criticized?
38. What are the effects of positive and negative transfers? Illustrate your answer with examples.

Projects

1. Make a summary of one of the contrastive topics in Khalil, A. 1996. A Contrastive Grammar of English and Arabic. Jerusalem: Al-Isra' Press.
2. Give two examples in each linguistic level for Arabic transfer in learning English by using Kharma, N. and A. Hajjaj. 1989. Errors

in English among Arabic Speakers: Analysis and Remedy. Essex: Longman Group Limited.
3. Collect and determine the source of at least ten grammatical errors from Noor, H. 1996. English syntactic errors by Arabic speaking learners: Reviewed. Pan-Asiatic, Volume, IV,1441–1465.
4. Give two examples for avoidance at different linguistic levels which are done by you or by one of your colleagues in class, or a student you know in public education.
5. Draw a table of distinction between CA and EA.

For Further Reading

Contrastive Analysis

Al-Shaikhli, M. F. & Abdel-Latif Shalabi, I. 2011. English–Arabic contrastive analysis redefinition of goals. *Journal of Language Teaching and Research*, 2, 1337–1345.

James, C. 1980. *Contrastive analysis*. Essex: Longman Group Limited.

Khalil, A. 1996. *A contrastive grammar of English and Arabic*. Jerusalem: Al-Isra' Press.

Kharma, N. 1983. *A Contrastive analysis of the use of verbs forms in English and Arabic*. Heidelberg: Julius Groos Verlag.

Mukattash, L. 1983. Contrasitive analysis, error analysis and learning difficulty. In Fisiak, J. (Ed.), Contrastive linguistics: Problems and prospects (pp. 333–348). Amsterdam: J. Benjamins Publishers.

Robinett, B. & Schachter, J (Eds.). 1983. *Second language learning: contrastive analysis, error analysis and related aspects*. Ann Arbor: The University of Michigan Press.

Error Analysis

Cherrington, R. 2004. Error analysis. In: M. Byram, (Ed.), *Routledge encyclopedia of language teaching and learning* (pp. 198–200). London/New York: Routledge.
James, C. 1998. *Errors in language learning and use: Exploring error analysis.* London/New York: Routledge.
Lennon, P. 1991. Error: Some problems of definition, identification, and distinction. *Applied Linguistics*, 12, 180–95.
Odlin, T. 1989. *Language transfer: cross-linguistic influence in language learning.* Cambridge: Cambridge University Press.
Robinett, B. & Schachter, J (Eds.). 1983. *Second language learning: contrastive analysis, error analysis and related asspects.* Ann Arbor: The University of Michigan Press.
Richards, J. (Ed.). 1984. *Error analysis: Perspectives of second language acquisition.* London: Longman Group Limited.
Spillner, B. 1991. *Error analysis: A comprehensive bibliography.* Amsterdam: John Benjamins.
Tylor, G. 1986. Errors and explanations. *Applied Linguistics,* 7, 144–66.

Interlanguage

Bardovi-Harlig, K. 1999. The interlanguage of interlanguage pragmatics: A research agenda for acquisitional pragmatics. *Language Learning,* 49:677–713.
Crookes, G. 1989. Planning and interlanguage variability. *Studies in Second Language Acquisition*, 11, 367–83.
Dulay, H. & Burt, M. 1977. Remarks on creativity in language acquisition. In M. Burt, H. Dulay, & M. Finocchiaro (Eds.), *Viewpoints on English as a second language* (pp. 95–126). New York: Regents.
Dulay, H., Burt, M. & Krashen, S. 1987. *Language two.* New York: Oxford University Press.
Selinker, L. 1992. *Rediscovering interlanguage.* London: Longman Group Limited.

References

Al-Qadi, N. 1992. The Acquisition of English Derivational Morphology by Arab Speakers: Empirical Testing. *Language Sciences* 14: 89–107.

Al-Qadi, N. 1997. Native-Arabic Speakers' Knowledge of English Verb Inflections. *JKAU: Edu. Sci.* 10:3–17.

Adjemian, C. 1976. On the Nature of Interlanguage Systems. *Language Learning* 26:297–320.

Bardovi-Harlig, K. 1999. The interlanguage of interlanguage pragmatics: a research agenda for acquisitional pragmatics. *Language Learning* 49:677–713.

Blum, S. and E. A. Levenston. 1978. Universals of Lexical Simplification. *Language Learning* 28:399–416.

Corder, S. 1967. The Significance of Learner's Errors. *IRAL* 4:161–170.

Corder, S. 1971. Describing the Language Learner's Language. *CILT Reports and Papers* 6:57–64.

Crookes, G. 1989. Planning and Interlanguage Variability. *Studies in Second Language Acquisition* 11:367–83.

Dechert, H.W. and M. Raupach (Eds.) 1989. *Transfer in Language Production*. Norwood, New Jersey: Ablex Publishing Copration.

Dulay, H. and M. Burt 1977. Remarks on creativity in language acquisition. In M. Burt, H. Dulay, and M. Finocchiaro (Eds.) *Viewpoints on English as a Second Language.* New York: Regents.

Dulay, H., M. Burt, and Krashen S. 1987. *Language Two.* New York: Oxford University Press.

Duskova, L. 1969. On the Sources of Errors in Foreign Language Learning. *IRAL* 7:11–36.

Eubank, L., L. Selinker, and S. Smith 1995. *The Current State of Interlanguage.* Amsterdam: John Benjamins.

Faerch, C, K. Haastrup, and R. Phillipson. 1984. *Learner Language and Language Learning.* Clevedon, England: Multilingual Matters.

Fries, C. 1945. *Teaching and Learning English as a Foreign Language.* Ann Arbor, Mich.: The University of Michigan Press.

Gass, S. 1979. Language Transfer and Grammatical Relations. *Language Learning* 29:327–344.

Gass, S. and L. Selinker 1992. *Language Transfer in Language Learning*. Amsterdam: John Bejamins.

George, H. 1972. *Common Errors in Language Learning*. Rowley, MA: Newbury House.

James, C. 1998. *Errors in Language Learning and Use: Exploring Error Analysis*. London: Longman.

Johnson, K. 2001. *An Introduction to Foreign Language Learning and Teaching*. London: Longman.

Kaplan, R.B. 2002. *The Oxford Handbook of Applied Linguistics*. Oxford University Press.

Kharma, N. 1983. *A Contrastive Analysis of the Use of Verbs Forms in English and Arabic*. Heidelberg: Julius Groos Verlag.

Kharma, N. and A. Hajjaj. 1989. *Errors in English among Arabic Speakers: Analysis and Remedy*. Essex: Longman Group Limited.

Kleinmann, H. 1977. Avoidance Behavior in Adult Second Language Acquisition. *Language Learning* 27:93–107.

Lado, R. 1957. *Linguistics across Cultures: Applied Linguistics for Language Teachers*. Ann Arbor, Mich.: The University of Michigan Press.

Lee, W. 1968. Thoughts on Contrastive Linguistics in the Context of Foreign Language Teaching. In Alatis, J. (ed.). *Contrastive Linguistics and its Pedagogical Implications*, 185–194. Washington, D.C.: Georgetown University.

Lennon, P. 1991. Error: some problems of definition, identification, and distinction. *Applied Linguistics* 12:180–95.

Markham, P. 1985. Contrastive Analysis and the Future of Second Language Education. *System* 13:25–29.

McLaughlin, B. 1987. *Theories of Second Language Learning*. London: Edward Arnold.

Nemser, W. 1971. Approximative Systems of Foreign Language Learners. *IRAL* 9:115–123.

Noor, H. H. 1994. Some Implications on the Role of the Mother Tongue in Second Language Acquisition. *Linguistica Communicatio*, Morocco, vol. 6/1&2:96–106.

Noor, H. H. 1996. English Syntactic Errors by Arabic Speaking Learners: Reviewed. The proceedings of *the 4th International Symposium on Language and Linguistics. Pan-Asiatic Linguistics*, Thailand, pp.1441–55.

Noor, H. H. 1997. Conditional Sentences in English and Arabic: A Contrastive Analysis. *Linguistica Communicatio*, Morocco, vol. 9/1&2.

Noor, H. H. 1999. Transfer in Using Conditional Sentences by Saudi Arabian Learners of English. *Drasat* published by Center of Scientific Researches, Jordan University.

Noor, H. H. 2007. Competency in First Language: Does it affect the quality of second language writing? *Drasat* published by Center of Scientific Researches, Jordan University, 2007.

Noor, H. H. 2009a. The Influence of L2 on the Syntactic Processing of L1. SJI (Scientific Journal International) *Journal of Literature, Language and Linguistics, Vol.1, Issue 1.* <http://www.scientific-journals.org/journals2007/j_of_language_and_literature.htm>.

Noor, H. H. 2009b. Positive effects of second language learning on the use of first language: A case study of Arab students' learning English. *Society & Change* Vol. III, No. 3:7–22., July-September 2009.

Noor, H. H. and M. O. Fallata 2010. An Investigation of some difficulties in idioms encountered by Saudi learners of English. *IJAES (International Journal of Arabic-English Studies)*, Vol. 11, pp. 147–174, Libairie du Liban Publishres, 2010.

Noor, H. H. and A. A. Dhebaib 2011. Strategies used in producing English lexical collocations by Saudi EFL learners. The proceedings of *The 1st International Conference on Foreign Language Teaching and Applied Linguistics, 5–7 May, 2011Sarajevo* (pp. 574–595).

Norrish, J. 1983. *Language Learners and their Errors*. London: Illustrations Macmillan Publishers Ltd.

Odlin, T. 1989. *Language Transfer*. Cambridge: Cambridge University Press.

Richards, J. 1985. *The Context of Language Teaching.* Cambridge: Cambridge University Press.
Richards, J., J. Paltt, and H. Weber. 1985. *Longman Dictionary of Applied Linguistics.* Essex. Longman Group Limited.
Schachter, J. 1974. An Error in Error Analysis. *Language Learning* 24: 205–214.
Schachter, J. 1979. Reflections on error production. *Interlanguage Studies Bulletin* 4:15–26.
Selinker, L. 1969. Language Transfer. *General Linguistics* 9:67–92.
Selinker, L. 1972. Interlanguage. *IRAL* 10:209–231.
Selinker, L. 1992. *Rediscovering Interlanguage.* London: Longman.
Selinker, L., J. Lamendella 1978. Two Perspectives on Fossilization in Interlanguage Learning. *Interlanguage Studies Bulletin* 3:143–191.
Sirdhar, S. 1980. Contrastive Analysis, Error Analysis and Interlanguage: Three Phases of One Goal. In Croft, K. (ed.). *Readings on English as a Second Language for Teachers and Teacher Trainees*, 91–119. Boston: Little, Brown and Company.
Spillner, B. 1991. *Error Analysis: A Comprehensive Bibliography.* Amsterdam: John Benjamins.
Stockwell, R., D. Bowen, and J. Martin. 1965. *The Grammatical Structures of English and Spanish.* Chicago: The University of Chicago Press.
Tarone, E. 1979. Interlanguage as Chameleon. *Language Learning* 29: 181–191.
Taylor, B. 1975. The Use of Overgeneralization and Transfer Learning Strategies by Elementary and Intermediate Students in ESL. *Language Learning* 25:73–107.
Tylor, G. 1986. Errors and explanations. *Applied Linguistics* 7:144–66.
Tran-Thi-Chau. 1975. Error Analysis, Contrastive Analysis, and Students' Perception: A Study of Difficulty in Second-language Learning. *IRAL* 13:119–143.
Van Els, T., T. Bongaerts, G. Extra, C. Van Os, and A. Dieten. 1984. *Applied Linguistics and the Learning and Teaching of Foreign Languages.* London: Edward Arnold.

Chapter 5: Non-Linguistic Factors In L2 Learning

This chapter deals with the most common non-linguistic factors affecting the L2 learning success:

1. Aptitude
2. Intelligence
3. Motivation
4. Anxiety
5. Personality
6. Age

5.1 Introduction

In the same environment, some learners learn an L2 better or faster than others. Although these learners are normal, i.e. they do not have any speech defects and have an innate ability to learn their L1 and one foreign language or more, certain individual characteristics affect their efficiency and speed of learning the L2. Gardner and Lambert (1959:272) found that maximum prediction of success in learning an L2 was obtained from tests of:

1. verbal intelligence,
2. intensity of motivation to learn the L2,
3. student's purpose in studying the L2, and
4. one index of linguistic aptitude.

The results of these four tests and some others are considered to be the non-linguistic factors affecting the learning success of an L2.

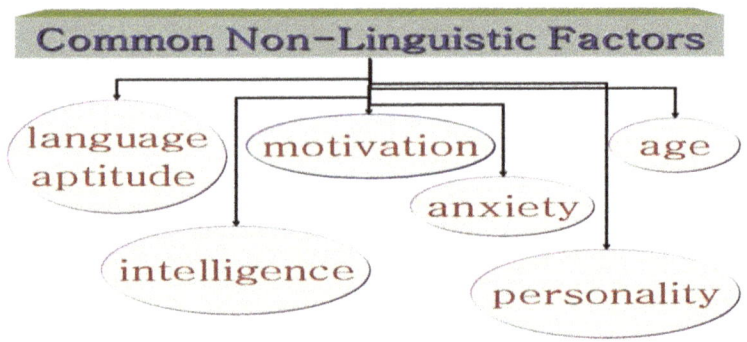

Figure 5.1: Common Non-Linguistic Factors.

In this chapter, the common non-linguistic factors will briefly be discussed by showing how they are related to success in L2 learning.

5.2 Language Aptitude

Language (or linguistic) aptitude is the natural ability to learn a language. This language aptitude in L2 includes various abilities, as in the following:

1. identification of sound patterns (i.e. the word 'he', for example, is composed of the consonant /h/ and the long vowel /i:/),
2. recognition of grammatical functions of words in sentences (i.e. the relationship that a word has in a sentence with the other words, such as that a word is the subject or the object of a verb),
3. inference of language rules, and
4. memory of language materials.

It is supposed that a learner with high language aptitude can learn more quickly and easily than a learner with low language aptitude. Skehan (1989:38) stated that "aptitude is consistently the best predictor of language learning success." Human beings have an innate ability for learning any language, i.e. the ability to constitute the linguistic knowledge of any language. It is logical to assume that every normal human being has some sort of language aptitude, but in varying degrees. The above–mentioned abilities of language aptitude are reasonable predictors of the L2 learning success. If a learner has all abilities or most of them, he has an advantage in learning an L2 (Gass and Selinker 1994:248). However, Carroll (1981:86) stated that *foreign language aptitude* is not considered the initial state of readiness and capacity for learning; it is relatively fixed over a long period of one's lifespan, and relatively hard to modify in any significant way. This shows that normal learners of different aptitudes can learn an L2 if they are given enough time.

5.3 Intelligence

Intelligence is defined as the good mental ability to learn and understand. This covers mind's capacities for abstract thought, understanding, communication, reasoning, learning, planning, and problem solving. Pimsleur, Mosberg and Morrison (1962:160) argued that underachievement, i.e. partial or complete failure in learning an L2 may not be the result of inferior mental ability of the learner, especially in the elementary stages. Wittich (1962:211) got a similar result in saying that "I.Q. (i.e. intelligence quotient) was the poorest single predictor of achievement in foreign languages." Carroll (1962:90) stated that intelligence tests are not largely considered in screening students for second/foreign learning training. This confirms that L2 underachievers are not inferior in mental ability, but their failure may be due to other non-linguistic factors.

5.4 Motivation

Motivation is the factor that determines a person's desire to do something. Desires or forces drive the learner towards the goals of the L2 program that he participates in. The motivated behaviour is the whole activity of L2 learning in and out of the classroom. The learners create the favorable feeling which supports them emotionally and psychologically in the learning process. There are two types of motivation in L2 learning:

1. *instrumental motivation*: learning an L2 can be a useful instrument to achieve other goals such as getting a job, gaining a necessary qualification or improving employment prospects.
2. *integrative motivation*: learning an L2 is for satisfactory communication in that L2 and having closer contact with its people and culture.

Gardner and Lambert (1972) found that learners with a higher integrative motivation are more likely to achieve greater proficiency. However, most L2 learners have a mixture of integrative and instrumental motivations. Gardner and Lambert (1972) and Lukmani (1972) found that the level of the learners' instrumental motivation correlates best with their success in L2 learning. In both studies, English is learnt as an international language, i.e. a language of international communication between people from different countries who do not speak each other's native language, or within a multilingual country such as India. When English is learnt primarily for its international function, *attitudes* towards the L2 community do not exert an important influence. Learners with positive attitudes or more favorable attitudes towards the L2 community wish for more intensive contact with the L2 native speakers. These attitudes make learners have integrative motivation, clear communicative need and finally good mastery over the L2. Negative attitudes towards the L2 community may make strong internal barriers against L2 learning, and if learning has to take place, it will proceed only to the minimum required level.

5.4.1 Factors Affecting Motivation

Intrinsic factors and extrinsic factors determine three general types of motivation (Carroll 1967:97). The intrinsic factors arise from learners themselves, whereas extrinsic factors come from school and its system, home and society. The three general motivation types are *positive, neutral and negative*. Learners begin in most cases with neutral or positive motivation, but rarely with negative motivation. Intrinsic factors instill confidence in the learner and help him achieve his goals in learning the L2. Extrinsic factors strengthen positive motivation in schools through good teachers, excellent textbooks and other facilities which may have a significant role, leading to favorable motivation. At home and in society, positive motivation is achieved by the encouragement of parents and other members of the family, and by the importance of the L2 in the society as a whole. Such extrinsic factors may transfer a neutral motivation into a positive motivation. Repeated success in the classroom leads to the creation of positive attitudes towards the L2 itself and makes the motivation positive. Bad experiences among family or members of society, such as the L2 is difficult to learn or there is no need to learn it, may lead to the creation of negative attitudes towards the L2 itself and makes the motivation negative. Another factor that contributes to negative motivation is the syndrome that results from failure in the form of repeated frustration inside the classroom. With such frustration, the learner begins to dislike the L2, its teacher, the school and himself (Hussein 1971:48). Different types of motivation in second language learning in general, indicate clearly that motivation is one of the most important factors in learning the L2.

5.5 Anxiety

Anxiety is an emotional condition where the learner feels insecure with the learning process. When the learner is anxious or even overanxious, there are likely to be psychological barriers to communication.

Anxiety is the result of personal factors. Some learners become anxious more quickly than others whatever the situation is. Other learners may have bad experiences with failure. This disappointment causes them to quickly become anxious. If anxiety arises above a certain level, it may be an obstacle to the language learning process. Typical classrooms can easily generate situations where learners feel anxious. For example, learners are asked to perform in a state of ignorance and dependence on their teachers. They produce unfamiliar sounds in front of an audience. When they do not perform adequately, they may be subjected to comments and corrections (or laughter). Sometimes, learners cannot figure out the reasons for the comments and corrections. Moreover, learners do not possess the linguistic tools in the L2 to help them express themselves; hence, the interaction is usually dominated by the teacher. A sympathetic teacher and co-operative atmosphere in the classroom may have a supportive effect to reduce learners' anxiety to an acceptable level. In conclusion, too much anxiety may hinder learning, but a certain amount of it can stimulate a learner to invest more energy in learning. This shows that the relationship between anxiety and learning is rather weak (Littlewood 1984:58–59, and Skehan 1989:115–118).

5.6 Personality

Personal characteristics are likely to influence L2 learning positively or negatively. However, this influence is supported by observation not by empirical studies, since it is not easy to demonstrate the link between the characteristics of personality and L2 learning (Littlewood 1984:64). The types of characteristics which are preferable in L2 learning are *extroversion and high self-esteem*. The non-preferable personality traits, which are the opposites of the preferable ones, are *introversion and egocentrism*.

Extroverts or outgoing learners are easily involved in social interactions both inside and outside the classroom, i.e. they obtain more language input and more practice in using an L2. Social interactions inside the classroom are very helpful in formal learning by getting more attention from their teachers and other learners. Outside the classroom, social interactions facilitate natural language learning. In contrast, introvert learners are more interested in their own thoughts and feelings rather in social interaction with other learners around them.

Learners with a high level of self-esteem are less likely to feel threatened when communicating in an L2 with which the learner feels strange in an unfamiliar situation. However, egocentric learners are self-conscious and they do not take risks in learning. Subconsciousness and risk-taking are necessary for rapid progress in L2 learning.

5.7 Age

It is commonly believed that children are faster than adults in learning foreign languages. Children can gain a high level of mastery over an L2, whereas adults cannot. Children acquiring an L2 in the L2 environment are more likely to sound like native speakers than adults are. Adults may appear to make greater progress initially, but children nearly always surpass them (Snow and Hoefnagle-Hohle 1978). The most common explanation for such observation is that there is a critical period during which the brain is flexible and learning can occur naturally and effortlessly. This period ends around puberty; hence, adolescents and adults show traces of foreignness in producing the L2 and the language learning process becomes artificial for them (see, for example, Oyama 1976, Seliger, Krashen, and Ladefoged 1975, and Asher and Garcia 1969). This shows that L2 learning success is related to whether learning is in the period of pre-puberty or post-puberty. There are, however, a number of adolescents and adults who are able to learn an L2 with a high level of proficiency. This means that these adolescents and adults have not lost their capacity of natural language learning. There is a general consensus that younger children are superior in pronunciation skills and they are more likely to achieve a native-like accent. However, older learners tend to develop morphological and syntactic elements of the L2 more quickly than younger learners. Researchers assign a number of reasons for such observational efficiency in language learning by younger learners over older learners:

1. Younger learners' brains retain plasticity[15] whereas older learners' lose it.
2. Children are exposed to simple language,[16] which is easier to process and understand, for longer periods of time.
3. Children receive more intensive attention from both adults and other children who are native speakers of the L2.
4. Children do not have barriers to interaction and learning the L2 since they do not hold negative attitudes towards native speakers of the L2 and are unaware of factors such as fear of rejection.
5. Children analyze the language they are learning less than adults. They are unconscious of the learning processes with which learning goes through in its proper course in a natural and easy way.
6. Children have a clear communicative need for learning an L2, such as watching TV in which the L2 is the language used, or playing with other children, with whom the L2 is the only form of communication.

---

[15] Neuroplasticity or brain plasticity refers to the brain's ability to change throughout life. The brain has the amazing ability to reorganize itself by forming new connections between brain cells (neurons), cf. Michelon, 2008, <http://sharpbrains.com/blog/2008/02/26/brain-plasticity-how-learning-changes-your-brain/>.

[16] Simple language basically comes from simple structure, short utterances, more limited vocabulary, reference to immediate situations, and more repetitions by children.

5.8 Conclusion

We have looked briefly at the most common non-linguistic factors which may relate to the success of L2 learning. Some of these non-linguistic factors have a somewhat measurable effect on learning an L2, like motivation and age. Others may have a weak effect, such as language aptitude, intelligence, anxiety and personality. All these factors, however, are complicated issues, interact in complex ways and affect L2 learning success. What is known and presented in studies about interactions with second language learning is still limited. Thus, the preferable conditions for learning an L2 are far from reach, and thus more reliable studies are needed.

Study Questions

1. Why are some learners better or faster than others in learning an L2?
2. What is 'language aptitude'?
3. What are the abilities of language aptitude?
4. Are abilities of language aptitude an advantage or a disadvantage in learning an L2, and why?
5. Define intelligence.
6. Is intelligence a good single predictor in learning an L2 or not, and why?
7. What is 'motivation'? Describe its two types in L2 learning.
8. Which type of motivation is better for learning an L2, and why?
9. Why does instrumental motivation lead to success in L2 learning when English is learned as an international language?
10. Why are positive attitudes towards the L2 community better while negative attitudes are worse in learning an L2?

11. What are the two factors that determine the three general types of motivation?
12. What are the three general types of motivation? Explain their relationship to the L2 learning success.
13. What is 'anxiety'?
14. Why do foreign learners feel anxious in the classroom?
15. What reduces learners' anxiety in the classroom to an acceptable level?
16. Why is a certain amount of anxiety in learning an L2 acceptable?
17. Why does too much anxiety hinder learning an L2?
18. What are the characteristics of a learner's personality that help in learning an L2, and why?
19. Why are children faster at learning an L2?
20. Who is better in learning pronunciation and who is better in early morphological and syntactic development?
21. What are the six reasons of efficiency in language learning by younger learners over older ones?
22. Classify the non-linguistic factors into two groups as measurable effects and weak effects on learning an L2.

Projects

1. Do you agree that foreign language aptitude is not considered the initial state of readiness and capacity for learning, and why?
2. From your experience in L2 learning, what are the reasons of L2 underachievement?
3. The motivation to learn an L2 is both in and out of the classroom. Give examples for both cases.
4. Explain the important influence of attitudes towards the L2 community when English is learned primarily as an international language.

5. Think of some reasons that may make the learner frustrated in the L2 classroom.
6. Give examples from real-life situations that a certain amount of 'anxiety' can stimulate a learner to invest more energy in learning.

For Further Reading

Brown, H. D. 1987. *Principles of language learning and teaching* (2nd ed.). Englewood Cliffs, New Jersey: Prentice-Hall, Inc.
Dulay, H., Burt, M. & Krashen, S. 1982. *Language two*. New York: Oxford University Press.
Ellis, R. 1994. *The study of second language acquisition*. New York: Oxford University Press.
Gardner, R. 1985. *Social psychology and second language learning: The role of attitudes and motivation*. London: Edward Arnold.
Trofimovich, P., Turuševa, L. & Gatbonton, E. 2013. Group membership and identity issues in second language learning. *Language Teaching*, 46, 563–567.
Sansone, C. & Harackiewicz, J. M. (Eds.). 2000. *Intrinsic and extrinsic motivation: The search for optimal motivation and performance*. London: Academic Press.
Singleton, D. 1989. *Language acquisition: The age factor*. Clevedon: Multilingual Matters.
Spolsky, B. 1989. *Conditions for second language learning*. New York. Oxford University Press.
Sasaki, M. 1999. *Second language proficiency, foreign language aptitude, and intelligence: Quantitative and qualitative analyses*. New York: Peter Lang Publishing Group.

References

Asher, J., and R. Garcia 1969. The Optimal Age to Learn a Foreign Language. *Modern Language Journal* 53:334–341.

Carroll, J. B. and S. Sapon 1959. *Modern Language Aptitude Test- Form A*. New York: The Psychological Corporation.

Carroll, J. 1962. The Prediction of Success in Intensive F. L. Training, In Glaser, R. (ed.), *Training Research and Education*. University of Pittsburgh.

Carroll, J. 1967. Research Problems Concerning the Teaching of Foreign or Second Language to Younger Children. In H. H. Stern (ed.), *Foreign Language in Primary Education*. New York: Oxford University Press.

Carroll, J. B. 1981. Twenty-five Years of Research on Foreign Language Aptitude. In Diller K.C. (ed.), *Individual Differences and Universals in Language Learning Aptitude*. Rowley, Mass: Newbury House.

Gardner, Robert C. and Lambert, Wallace E. 1959. Motivational Variables in Second Language Acquisition. *Canadian Journal of Psychology* 13:266–272.

Gardner, R. C. and W. Lambert 1972. *Attitudes and Motivation in Second Language Learning*. Rowley, Mass.: Newbury House.

Gass, S. and L. Selinker 1994. *Second Language Acquisition: An Introductory Course*. Hillsdale, New Jersey: Lawrence Erlbaum Associates, Inc.

Hussein, A. I. 1971. Remedial English for Speakers of Arabic: A Psycholinguistic Approach. (Unpublished Ph.D Dissertation). The University of Texas at Austin.

Littlewood, W. 1984. *Foreign and Second Language Learning*. Cambridge: Cambridge University Press.

Lukmani, Y. 1972. Motivation to Learn and Language Proficiency. *Language Learning* 22:261–273.

Oyama, S. 1976. A Sensitive Period for the Acquisition of a Non-Native Phonological System. *Journal of Psycholinguistic Research* 5:61–285.

Pimsleur, P., L. Mosberg, and A. Morrison 1962. Student Factors in Foreign Language Learning. *Modern Language Journal* 46:60–170.

Robinson, P. 2001. *Cognition and Second Language Instruction.* Cambridge: CUP.

Selinger, H. S. Krashen, and P. Ladefoged 1975. Maturational Constraints in the Acquisition of a Native-Like Accent, *Second Language Learning. Language Sciences* 36:20–22.

Skehan. P. 1989. *Individual Differences in Second-Language Learning.* London: Edward Arnold.

Snow, C. and M. Hoefnagle-Hohle 1978. The Critical Age for Second Language Acquisition: Evidence from Second Language Learning. *Child Development* 49:1114–1128.

Wittich, Barbara Von. 1962. Prediction of Success in Foreign Language Study. *Modern Language Journal* 5:208–212. <http://sharpbrains.com/blog/2008/02/26/brain-plasticity-how-learning-changes-your-brain/>.

Chapter 6: Language Learning Strategies

This chapter discusses the following topics in detail:

1. the common language learning strategies that help EFL/ESL learners overcome learning problems,
2. characteristics and types of learning strategies,
3. the factors that affect strategy choice, and
4. views of researchers regarding the effect of strategy training in language teaching.

6.1 Introduction

Research in the area of language learning strategies provides us with some information about learners' perception of what to do to learn or to manage their learning. It demonstrates that L2 learning strategies play a significant role in the learning process. These strategies can be taught, and acquiring them can make a substantial difference in learner achievement. Ellis (1994:529), for example, has shown that individual learner differences together with various situational factors determine learner's choice of learning strategies (Figure 6.1). Learning strategies, in turn, influence two aspects of learning: the rate of acquisition and the ultimate level of achievement. Furthermore, the learners' level of L2 proficiency and their language success can also affect the choice of strategies.

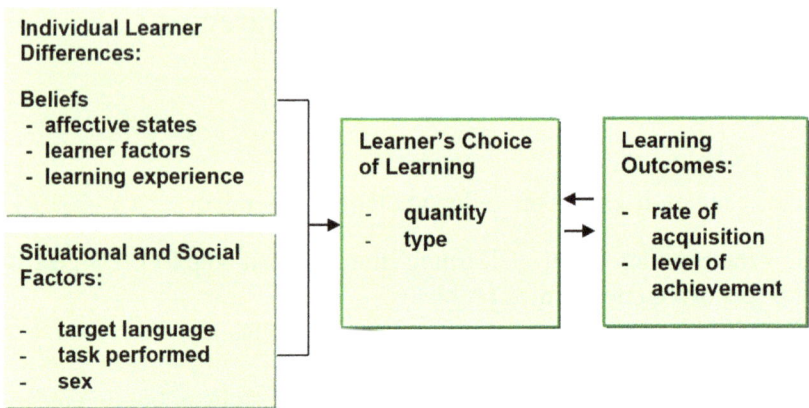

Figure 6.1: The relationship between individual learner differences, situational factors, learning strategies, and learning outcomes (Ellis 1994:530).

6.2 Definitions of Learning Strategies

The notion of strategies has been controversial amongst applied linguists. In studies, such as those mentioned in Table 6.1 below, strategies have been referred to as techniques, tactics, conscious plans, learning skills, cognitive abilities, language processing strategies, problem-solving procedures, etc.[17] To better understand some of the problems involved in arriving at consensus concerning the notion of strategies, let us look at some attempts to define language learning strategies (Table 6.1).

---

17   For a discussion of the notion 'strategies', see Cohen 1998; Chapter 2 'Second Language Learning and Language Use Strategies: defining terms.'

Table 6.1: Definitions of Learning Strategies.

Source	Definition
O'Malley et al. (1985)	'Learning strategies have been broadly defined as any set of operations or steps used by a learner that will facilitate the acquisition, storage, retrieval or use of information.'
Charmot (1987)	'Learning strategies are techniques, approaches or deliberate actions that students take in order to facilitate the learning, recall of both linguistic and content area information.'
Rubin (1987)	'[...] learner strategies include any set of operations, steps, plans, routines used by the learner to facilitate the obtaining, storage, retrieval, and use of information.'
Oxford (1989)	'Language learning strategies are behaviors or actions which learners use to make language learning more successful, self-directed, and enjoyable.'
Cohen (1998)	'[...] those processes which are consciously selected by learners and which may result in action taken to enhance the learning or use of a second or foreign language, through the storage, retention, recall, and application of information about the language.'

The definitions quoted above reveal problems concerning the nature of strategies. The researchers seem to disagree as to whether the strategies are observable behavior or mental operations. It is also disputable as to what kind of contribution they make to SLA, what might prompt language learners to use strategies, and finally whether strategies are more general in their use or tied to specific learning content and tasks. However, researchers, such as those mentioned in the definitions in table 6.1, seem to agree regarding the problem-solving and intentional nature of strategies as well as their facilitating function in the learning process. Wenden (1987:7) for example, emphasizes that learner strategies should include 'what learners know about the strategies they use', i.e. their strategic knowledge, and 'aspects of their language learning other than the strategies they use', e.g. personal factors facilitating learning, general language learning principles, etc. Also Oxford (1990:1) points out the importance of strategies for language learners as "tools for active, self-directed involvement, which are essential for developing communicative competence." She adds that "appropriate learning strategies result in improved proficiency and greater self-confidence." Moreover, Cohen (1998:5) showed the importance of taking both L2 learning and L2 use strategies into account when speaking about language learning strategies. He emphasizes that these strategies should aid the learner with the means to identify the material that requires more effort to learn, i.e. those materials which are more important than other materials should be grouped together for easier learning and then committed to memory.

6.3 Characteristics of Language Learning Strategies

Several researchers, in an attempt to define learning strategies, tried to compile a list of their main characteristics (cf. Wenden 1987:7; Oxford 1990:8–13; Bilystock 1990:12; Ellis 1994:532–33; Drozdzial-Szelest 1997:30–31). The next list represents the main characteristics of language learning strategies which learners develop to overcome some particular learning problems and their examples are shown in Table 6.2.

1. Strategies involve linguistic behavior (such as requesting the name of an object) and non-linguistic behavior (such as pointing at an object so as to be told its name).
2. Some strategies are behavioral (directly observable such as repetition of some words or language items for the sake of better pronunciation or recognition, etc.), while others are mental (not directly observable such as internalization of items of language, etc).
3. Strategies are behavior which is amenable to change; they can be modified, rejected; new strategies can be learned/taught.
4. Strategies are systematic; learners uncover the strategy from their knowledge of the problem and employ it systematically.
5. Strategies contribute indirectly to learning by providing learners with data about the L2 which they can then process. However,

some strategies may also contribute directly, as in memorization strategies directed at specific lexical items or grammatical rules.
6. Strategy use or communicative strategies vary considerably as a result of both the kinds of task the learner is engaged in and individual learner preferences.

6.4 Types of Language Learning Strategies

Two taxonomies deserve special attention as they both contribute to our knowledge of learning strategies: O'Malley et al. and Oxford.

6.4.1 O'Malley et al.'s Framework

O'Malley and his colleagues, in extensive research based on cognitive psychology, studied the use of learning strategies by learners of English as an L2 in the USA (O'Malley et al. 1985a,b; Chamot 1987; Chamot and O'Malley 1987; O'Malley et al. 1989; O'Malley and Chamot 1990). O'Malley and his colleagues defined three main types of strategies used by L2 students:

1. *Metacognitive strategies* are executive skills that involve planning and thinking about learning, monitoring or evaluating the success of a learning activity.
2. *Cognitive strategies* are more directly related to individual learning tasks and entail direct manipulation or transformation of the learning materials in ways that enhance learning.
3. Social strategies refer to learning by interacting with other people.

The three types of strategies are described in Table 6.2.

Table 6.2: O'Malley et al. "Classification of Learning Strategies" (1985b:582–84).

Learning Strategy	Description
Metacognitive strategies	
Advanced organizers	Making a general but comprehensive preview of the organizing concept or principle in an anticipated activity.
Directed attention	Deciding in advance to attend to a learning task and to ignore irrelevant distracters.
Selective attention	Deciding in advance to attend to specific aspects of language input.
Self-management	Understanding the conditions that help one to learn and arranging for the presence of those conditions.
Functional planning	Planning for and preparing oneself for any necessity.
Self-monitoring	Correcting one's speech for accuracy in pronunciation, grammar, vocabulary, or for appropriateness as related to the setting or the people who are present.
Delayed production	Consciously deciding to postpone speaking in order to learn initially through listening comprehension.
Self-evaluation	Checking the outcome of one's own language learning against an internal measure of completeness and accuracy.
Cognitive Strategies	
Repetition	Imitating a language model, including overt practice and silent rehearsal.
Resourcing	Using the L2 reference materials.
Translation	Using the L1 as a base for understanding and/or producing the L2.
Grouping	Reordering or reclassifying, and perhaps labeling the material to be learned based on common attributes.
Note taking	Writing down the main idea, important points, outline, or summary of information presented orally or in writing.
Deduction	Consciously applying rules to produce or understand the L2.
Recombination	Constructing a meaningful sentence or larger language sequence by combining the known elements in a new way.

Learning Strategy	Description
Imagery	Relating new information to visual concepts in memory via familiar, easily retrievable visualizations, phrases, or locations.
Auditory representation	Retention of the sound or a similar sound for a word, phrase, or larger sequences.
Keyword	Remembering a new word in the L2 by (1) identifying a familiar word in the L1 that sounds like or otherwise resembles the new word (Transfer), and (2) generating easily recalled images of some relationship between the new word and the familiar word (Overgeneralization).
Contextualization	Putting a word or phrase in a meaningful language sequence.
Elaboration	Relating new information to other concepts in memory.
Transfer	Using previously acquired linguistic and/or conceptual knowledge to facilitate a new language learning task.
Inferencing	Using available information to guess meanings of new items, predict outcomes or fill in missing information.
Social Strategies	
Cooperation	Working with one or more peers to obtain feedback, pool information, or model a language activity.
Question for clarification	Asking a teacher, a peer or a native speaker for repetition, paraphrasing, explanation and/or examples.

The type of strategy varies according to the task the students are engaged in. For example, a listening task leads to the metacognitive strategies of selective attention and problem identification as well as self-monitoring. Also involved are the cognitive strategies of note taking, inferencing and memorizing along with elaboration. A vocabulary task calls forth the metacognitive strategies of self-monitoring and self-evaluation, and the cognitive strategies of sourcing and elaboration. The use of strategies also varies according to students' level: for example, intermediate students use slightly less strategies in total, but proportionately more metacognitive strategies (cf. O'Malley and Chamot, 1990).

6.4.2 Oxford's Classification

Oxford attempted to subsume within her taxonomy, all strategies that have been mentioned in the literature on the subject. Oxford (1990) draws a distinction between two major classes of strategies: direct and indirect as shown in Figure 6.2. The former consists of 'strategies that are directly involved in the L2 in the sense that they require mental processing of the language' (1990:37), while the latter 'provides indirect support for language learning through focusing, planning, evaluating, seeking opportunities, controlling anxiety, increasing cooperation and empathy and other means' (1990:151).

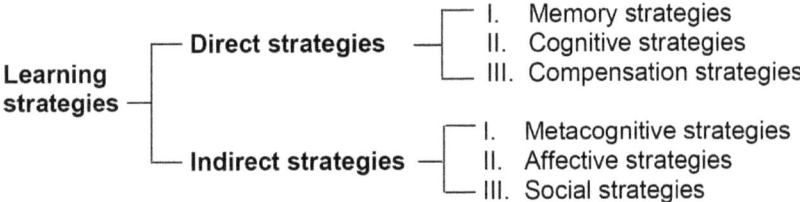

Figure 6.2: Diagram of the strategy system (Oxford 1990:16).

As can easily be seen, this distinction is parallel to O'Malley et al.'s distinction between *cognitive* and *metacognitive strategies* respectively. Both direct and indirect strategies provide support for one another and are applicable to all language skills.

Direct strategies include memory strategies (for remembering and retrieving new information), *cognitive strategies* (for understanding and producing the language), and *compensation strategies* (for using the language to make up for the lack of relevant knowledge). **Indirect strategies** are divided into *metacognitive strategies* (for coordinating the learning process), *affective strategies* (for regulating emotions), and *social strategies* (for learning with others) (cf. Oxford 1990:14–15). The six strategy groups are subdivided into further strategy sets as illustrated below (Figure 6.3) and these, in turn, are broken down into further levels.

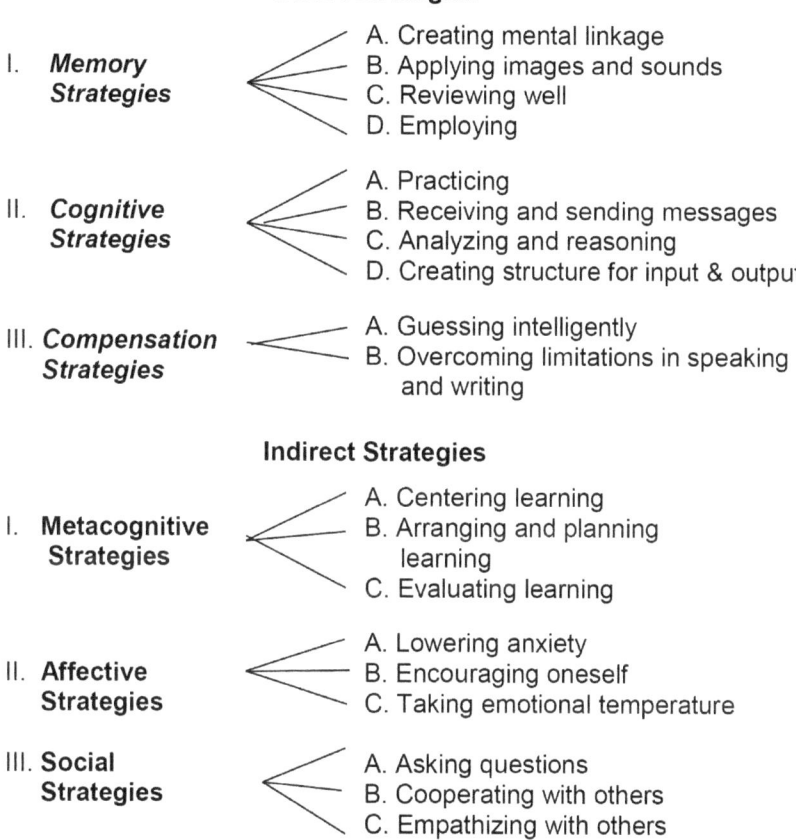

Figure 6.3: Diagram of the strategy system: Direct and Indirect strategy groups and sets (Oxford 1990:17).

Oxford observes that strategies used by language learners change with the level of proficiency, and that they may be directed at developing particular aspects of communicative competence. For example, learners may use cognitive strategies for reasoning deductively and may use contrastive analysis to improve their grammatical accuracy, or they may employ social strategies, such as asking questions or cooperating with other peers or native speakers to aid their sociolinguistic competence.

6.5 Factors Affecting Strategy Choice

Learners have been found to vary considerably in both the overall frequency with which they employ strategies and also the particular types of strategies they use. Here, we consider the range of factors that have been found to affect strategy choice. Some of these factors were discussed in Chapter 5 as part of the non-linguistic factors that affect L2 learning. These factors are:

6.5.1 Age

Age emerges as a clear factor affecting the way strategies are used. Young children have been observed to employ strategies in a task-specific manner, while older children and adults make use of generalized strategies, which they employ more flexibly. Young children's strategies are often simple, while mature learners' strategies are more complex and sophisticated. These differences may help explain why older children, adolescents and adults generally learn faster initially than young children and also why this advantage is more evident in grammar and vocabulary, for which there are many learning strategies, rather than pronunciation, for which there are few.

6.5.2 Aptitude

Aptitude does not appear to be strongly related to strategy use. Leino (1982) found that learners with high conceptual levels were better at describing their strategies than learners with low conceptual levels. It is possible, then, that learning strategies are related to that part of language aptitude shared with a general intelligence factor.

6.5.3 Motivation

Highly-motivated learners were found to use more strategies relating to formal practice, functional practice, general study, and conversation/input elicitation than poorly motivated learners (Oxford,1990). The type of motivation may also influence strategy choice. For example, employing integrative motivation can result in a preference for more communication-oriented strategies.

6.5.4 Personality

It has been found that there is a close relationship between personality types and strategy choice. For example, extrovert learners are credited with a willingness to take risks, but with dependency on outside stimulation and interaction. Extrovert leaners also reported significantly greater use of strategies that involved searching for and communicating meaning than did introverts.

6.5.5 The Learner's Personal Background

There is considerable evidence to support a link between learners' personal backgrounds and strategy use. For example, Ehrman (1990) found that students with at least five years of study reported using more functional practice strategies than students with four years or fewer. Also, Chamot et al. (1988) found that novice high school learners of a foreign language (FL) were likely to panic when they realized they lacked procedural skills for solving a language problem. On the other hand, expert learners (who had studied another FL previously) approached tasks calmly and were able to employ the strategies they had developed elsewhere.

6.5.6 Situational and Social Factors

Situational factors refer to the language being learned, the setting in which learning takes place, and the tasks that the learner is asked to perform. A number of differences between the learning strategies used by learners in a classroom as opposed to those used in a more natural setting have been found. Studies of classroom learners suggested that social strategies (such as questioning for clarification, cooperation, etc.) are rare. It is likely, however, that in many classrooms the kind of interaction that takes place affords little opportunity for the use of social strategies.

The research has also shown that task type had an influence on learners' choice of both cognitive and metacognitive strategies (see 6.4.1). For example, Chamot et al. (1987 and 1988) found that vocabulary tasks led to the use of the cognitive strategies of 'resourcing' and 'elaboration' and the metacognitive strategies of 'self-monitoring' and 'self-evaluation'. Listening tasks, on the other hand, led to 'note-taking', 'elaboration', 'inferencing', and 'summarizing' as cognitive strategies, and 'selective attention', 'self-monitoring', and 'problem-identification' as metacognitive strategies.

6.6 The Strategies of Good Language Learners

For more than two decades, L2 teachers and researchers alike have been interested in the factors accounting for success in learning an L2. The question why some language learners succeed in their efforts while others are doomed to failure in seemingly identical teaching contexts has been asked over and over again. Many studies have been carried out to find what learners who were known to be good at learning languages have in common. For example, Naiman et al. (1978) found the following broad strategies which were shared by good language learners:

1) *The learner finds a learning style that suits him.*
   Good language learners become aware of the style of L2 learning that suits them best. For example, some good language learners supplement audiolingual or communicative language teaching and/or learning by reading grammar books at home or listening to conversations by native speakers of the L2. Others seek out communicative encounters to help them compensate for a classroom with an academic emphasis.
2) *The learner involves himself in the language learning process.*
   Good language learners participate more in the classroom, whether visibly or not. They take the initiative and devise situations and language learning techniques for learning. Some listen to the news in the L2 on the radio or TV; others read books of fiction in the L2.
3) *The learners develop an awareness of language both as a system and as communication.*
   Good language learners treat language both as communication and as academic knowledge. For example, we can see that while some learners learn lists of vocabulary consciously (academic knowledge), others seek out opportunities to take part in conversations in the L2, i.e. communication.
4) *The learner pays constant attention to expanding his language knowledge.*
   Good language learners always make guesses about things they do not know. For example, they check whether they are right or wrong by comparing their speech with the new language they hear and also by asking native speakers to correct them. Some are continually on the lookout for clues to the L2.
5) The learner takes into account the demands that L2 learning imposes.
   The good language learner realizes that L2 learning is very demanding. It requires that he make much effort and pay more attention inside and outside the classroom in order to learn the L2.

Rubin and Thompson (1982) later added the following points to this list of good language learners:

1) living with uncertainty and developing strategies for making sense of the L2 without caring to understand every word.
2) using mnemonics (rhymes, word associations, etc.) to recall what has been learned.
3) making use of their errors to discover the L2 and to make inferences of its rules.
4) using linguistic knowledge, including knowledge of their L1 in mastering an L2.
5) learning different styles of speech and writing and learning to vary their language according to the formality of the situation.

6.7 Language Learning Strategies & Language Teaching

Strategy training has been emphasized by many researchers (e.g. Cook 1982; 2001; Bialystok 1990; Oxford 1990; O'Malley and Chamot 1990). These researchers argue in favor of such training that helps the learners to be aware of strategies in general rather than teaching them specific strategies. It is the learners' involvement, the learners' strategies, and the learners' ability to select their own ways that count, regardless of what the teacher is trying to do. The learners in general, must be encouraged to develop independence inside and outside the classroom. The following are the main points that may help the teacher to better train his/her students to take on responsibility for their learning (Cook 2001:106–08).

1) The teacher may exploit good language learning strategies with his students and make them aware of these strategies, so that they can choose the ones which suit them.
2) The teacher may train his students to develop their learning independence.
3) The teacher may make his students aware of a range of strategies that they can adopt.

4) The teacher may explain to his/her students similarities and differences between learning an L2 and learning other school subjects. Students in learning both an L2 and other school subjects, may be trained how to prepare themselves for the class, take notes, pay attention to what is said in the classroom, etc. These are general strategies useful for the students whether they are studying Physics or English.

6.8 Conclusion

The aim of this chapter is to aid language teachers in better understanding various types of learning strategies their students may adopt. We have looked briefly at the relationship between individual learner differences, situational factors, learning strategies, and learning outcomes. We came across different factors affecting the choice of language learning strategies, such as age, aptitude, motivation, personality, the learner's personal background, and the situational and social factors. Finally, we have shed some light on the good language learning strategies. We found that learners may vary in choosing their own strategies that may suit their needs and satisfaction.

Study Questions

1. What are the characteristics of learning strategies?
2. From the definitions of learning strategies you studied in this chapter, choose the one that you think covers most of the characteristics of these strategies and why?
3. What are the three types of strategies that O'Malley and his colleagues suggested in their framework of learning strategies?

4. What types of strategies do vocabulary tasks call for according to O'Malley et al.'s framework?
5. How does Oxford classify learning strategies?
6. Give examples of memory strategies.
7. Give examples of cognitive strategies.
8. Give examples of compensation strategies.
9. What is the factor that affects strategy choice most? Explain with examples.
10. In what ways does personal background affect learning strategies?
11. Do you think the setting in which learning takes place affects the choice of learning strategies?
12. Re-order Naiman et al.'s language learning strategies that are shared by good language learners according to your own point of view, from the most related or important to the least related or important.
13. Suppose you have a new lesson in grammar (particularly in tenses), what type of language learning strategy or strategies are you going to use?
14. Imagine that you are a teacher, what steps are you going to follow in order to train your students to take on responsibilities for their own learning?

Projects

1. From the different classifications of learning strategies you have studied here, can you think of your own classification?
2. Can you add to the characteristics of the good learner mentioned here in this chapter?
3. If you find different characteristics than those mentioned here, can you discern which ones are the most suitable for men and for women?

For Further Reading

Learning strategies are treated in depth by

Bialystok, E. 1990. *Communication Strategies: A Psychological Analysis of Second Language Use.* Oxford: Basil Blackwell.
Cohen, A. D. 1998. *Strategies in Learning and Using a Second Language.* Longman, New York.
Drozdzial-Syelest, K. 1997. *Language Learning Strategies in the Process of acquiring A Foreign Language.* Motivex Poynan: Poland.
O'Malley, J. and A. Chamot. 1990. *Learning Strategies in Second Language Acquisition.* Cambridge: Cambridge University Press.
Oxford, R. 1990. *Language Learning Strategies: What every teacher should know.* Newbury House/Harper & Row, New York.
Skehan, P. 1989. Language learning strategies (Chapter 5). *Individual Differences in Second-Language Learning* (pp. 73–99). London: Edward Arnold.
Weinstein, C., and R. Mayer 1986. The teaching of learning strategies. In M.C. Wittrock (Ed.), *Handbook of Research on Teaching*, 3rd Edition (pp. 315–327). New York: Macmillan.
Weinstein, C., E. Goetz, and P. Alexander (Eds.). 1988. *Learning and Study Strategies: Issues in Assessment, Instruction, and Evaluation.* New York: Academic Press.
Wenden, A. and J. Rubin (eds.) 1987. *Learner Strategies in Language Learning.* Englewood Cliffs, N.J.: Prentice Hall. Englewood Cliffs, N.J.

Factors Affecting Strategy Choice

Ellis, R. 1994. *The Study of Second Language Acquisition* (Part Five). Oxford, Oxford University Press.
Faerch, C. S. K. Haatrup, and R. Phillipson, 1984. *Learner Language and Language Learning* (Chapter twelve). Clevedon, Multilingual Matters Ltd.

Harley, B. 1986. *Age Factor in Second Language Acquisition*. Clevedon, Multilingual Matters Ltd.
Skehan, P. 1989. Language learning strategies (Chapter 5). *Individual Differences in Second-Language Learning* (pp. 73- 99). London: Edward Arnold.

Strategies of Good Language Learners

Naiman, N., M. Fröhlich, and A. Todesco, 1975. The good language learner. *TESL Talk* 6:58–75.
Rubin, J. 1975. What the 'good language learner' can teach us. *TESOL Quarterly*, 9/1:41–51.
Cook, V. J. 2001. *Linguistics and Second Language Acquisition*. St. Martin's Press, NY. (pp. 127–133).
Tarone, E. and G. Yule, 1989. *Focus on the Language Learner* (pp. 103–120). Oxford: Oxford University Press.

References

Bialystok, E. 1990. *Communication Strategies: A Psychological Analysis of Second-Language Use*. Oxford: Basil Blackwell.
Chamot, A. 1987. 'The learning strategies of ESL students' in Wenden and Rubin (eds.) 1987.
Chamot, A., L. Kupper, and M. Impink-Hernandez. 1988. *A Study of Learning Strategies in Foreign Language Instruction: Findings of the Longitudinal Study*. McLean, Va.: Interstate Research Associates.
Chamot, A., and M. O'Malley 1996. Implementing the cognitive academic language learning approach (CALLA). In R. Oxford (Ed.), *Language Learning Strategies Around the World: Cross-cultural*

Perspectives (pp. 167–173). Honolulu: University of Hawaii, Second Language Teaching and Curriculum Center

Cohen, A. D. 1998. Strategies in Learning and Using A Second Language. London: Longman.

Cook, V. 2001. *Second Language Learning and Language Teaching.* London: Arnold.

Davis, R. 1997. Modeling the strategies we advocate. *TESOL Journal*, 6(4), 5–6.

Drozdzial-Syelest, K. 1997. *Language Learning Strategies in the Process of Acquiring A Foreign Language.* Motivex Poynan: Poland.

Ehrman, M. 1990. 'The role of personality type in adult language learning: an ongoing investigation' in Parry and Stansfield (eds.) 1990.

Ellis, R. 1994. *The Study of Second Language Acquisition.* Oxford: Oxford University Press.

Leino, A. 1982. 'Learning process in terms of styles and strategies'. Research Bulletin No. 59. Helsinki, Finland.

LoCastro, V. 1994. Learning strategies and learning environments. *TESOL Quarterly*, 28(2), 409–414.

Naiman, N., M. Frohlich, H. Stern, and A. Todesco. 1978. *The Good Language Learner.* Research in Education Series No 7. Toronto: The Ontario Institute for Studies in Education.

Noor, H. H. 1996. Strategies in the acquisition of temporal clauses by EFL Arab learners. *Journal of King Abdulaziz University Educational Sciences*, Jeddah, Saudi Arabia, vol. 9:61–76.

Noor, H. H. and A. A. Dhebaib 2011. Strategies used in producing English lexical collocations by Saudi EFL learners. The proceedings of *The 1st International Conference on Foreign Language Teaching and Applied Linguistics, 5–7 May, 2011 Sarajevo* (pp. 574–595).

O'Malley, J., A. Chamot, G. Stewner-Manzanaraes, L. Kupper, and R. Russo. 1985a. 'Learning strategies used by beginning and intermediate ESL students'. *Language Learning* 35:21–46.

O'Malley, J., A. Chamot, G. Stewner-Manzanaraes, R. Russo, and L. Kupper. 1985b. 'Learning strategy applications with students of English as a second language'. *TESOL Quarterly* 19:285–96.

O'Malley, S. M., Chamot, A. U. and Kupper, L. 1989. 'Listening comprehension strategies in second language acquisition'. *Applied Linguistics* 10/4:418–37.

O'Malley, J. and A. Chamot. 1990. *Learning Strategies in Second Language Acquisition.* Cambridge: Cambridge University Press.

Oxford, R. L. 1989. 'Use of language learning: a synthesis of studies with implications for strategy training'. *System* 17/2/:255–67.

Oxford, R. 1990. *Language Learning Strategies: What Every Teacher Should Know.* Rowley, Mass.: Newbury House.

Rubin, J. 1987. 'Learner strategies: theoretical assumptions, research history and topology'. In Wenden, A. L. and Rubin, J. (eds.) pp. 15–30.

Rubin, J. and Thompson, I. 1982. *How to be A More Successful Learner.* Boston: Heinle and Heinle.

Wenden, A. 1987. 'How to be a successful learner: insights and prescriptions from L2 learners' in Wenden and Rubin (eds.) 1987.

Wenden, A. and J. Rubin (eds.) 1987. *Learner Strategies in Language Learning.* Englewood Cliffs, N.J.: Prentice Hall. Englewood Cliffs,N.J.

Glossary

Acculturation
Acculturation is the process of adapting to a new culture. This involves developing an understanding of the systems of thoughts, beliefs, and emotions of the new culture as well as its system of communication.

Anthropological Linguistics
A branch of linguistics which studies language variation and use in relation to the cultural patterns and beliefs of man, as investigated using the theories and methods of anthropology. For example, it studies the way in which linguistic features may identify a member of a (usually primitive) community with a social, religious, occupational or kinship group.

Anxiety
An emotional condition in which there is fear and uncertainty about the future. In SLA, anxiety may be both facilitating (i.e. it has a positive effect on L2 acquisition), or impeding (i.e. it has a negative effect).

Aphasia
It refers to partial or complete loss of the ability to use spoken language as a result of maldevelopment, disease or injury to the brain.

Approximative System
This term used by Nemser 1971 to refer to the deviant linguistic system which the learner employs when trying to use the L2. The learner passes through a number of 'approximative systems' on the way to acquiring full L2 proficiency.

Aptitude
Aptitude refers to the specific ability a learner has for learning an L2. This is hypothesized to be separate from the general ability to master academic skills, which is referred to as 'intelligence'.

Attitudes
What speakers of different languages have towards each other's languages. Attitudes towards a language may also show what people feel about the speakers of that language.

Avoidance
When speaking or writing an L2, a learner will often try to avoid using a difficult word or structure, and will use a simpler word or structure instead. This is called an avoidance strategy.

Behaviorism
A predominantly American learning theory developed earlier in the 20th century and associated with psychologists like Thorndike and Skinner. Learning is viewed as the development of stimulus-response associations through habit-formation, habits being developed by practice and reinforcement. Behaviorism had a strong effect on both linguistics (in particular structuralism) and language teaching, with audiolingualism attempting to apply its tenets.

Cognition
The various mental processes used in thinking, remembering, perceiving, recognizing, classifying, etc.

Cognitive Development
In this view, according to the cognitists, there is no innately predetermined language faculty. Instead, knowledge of language is just one of the results of more general mental abilities which enable humans to construct mental representations of the world. Knowledge of language grows as the child's mental abilities grow, this being the effect of the child interacting with his or her environment.

Cognitive Strategies
They are strategies that 'operate directly on incoming information, manipulating it in ways that enhance learning' (O'Mally and Chamot, 1990:44). These strategies involve such operations as rehearsal, organizing information, and inferencing.

Competence & Performance
Competence is the system of phonological, morphological, semantic, syntactic and lexical rules – a formal grammar – acquired, or internalized, by a native speaker during the language acquisition process in early childhood. It underlies his or her ability to produce and understand the sentences of a given language, and identify ambiguous and deviant sentences.

Performance is the production of utterances in specific situations. It depends additionally on memory limitations, as in the case of the production and the comprehension of extremely long sentences, social conventions, as in the case of the use of formal and information linguistic expressions, personality, interests, tiredness, and other diverse non-linguistic factors. Thus, competence is an idealization of, or an abstraction from, linguistic performance.

Concept
The general idea or meaning which is associated with a word or symbol in a person's mind. Concepts are the abstract meanings which words and other linguistic items represent.

Contrastive Analysis (CA)
It is to identify and catalogue the structural similarities and differences mainly between the native language and the L2. Such similarities and differences may predict what is easy and what is difficult in learning the L2. The difficulties are caused by interference from the native language. With the knowledge of difficulties, the teacher is ready to prevent or reduce such interference (i.e. L1 transfer) by drills, exercises, assignments, revisions, etc.

Critical Period Hypothesis
The Critical Period Hypothesis claims that there is a stage in the maturation of a human being during which language acquisition is possible in a natural fashion; before and after this period, true language acquisition cannot take place. This agrees with the popular notion that children are able to learn L2s successfully while adults are not.

Deep Structure
The deep structure is much more abstract than the surface structure and is considered to be in the speaker's, writer's, hearer's or reader's mind.

Egocentrism
Systematic selfishness, a state of mind in which one is always thinking of oneself.

Error Analysis (EA)
The study and analysis of the errors made by L2 learners. Such knowledge aids in the preparation of teaching material and teaching itself.

Errors
The application of L2 rules which do not correspond to L2 norms, resulting from incomplete acquisition. Such errors take time to be corrected. These errors may not be recognized by learners and they are committed at all linguistic levels: phonological, morphological, syntactic and semantic.

Extroversion/Introversion
These terms describe the dimension of personality which has been most thoroughly investigated in SLA research. They reflect a continuum: at one end are learners who are sociable and risk-takers, while at the other end are learners who are quiet and avoid excitement.

Filter
Learners do not necessarily attend to all the input they are exposed to. Rather they attend to some features, but 'filter' others out. Dulay et al. (1982) suggested that the use of the filter depends upon affective factors such as the learner's motives, attitudes, and emotions.

First/Native Language
The first or native language (L1/NL) which is normally acquired by a human being in early childhood through interaction with other members of his speech community. The alternative terms to L1/NL are primary language and mother tongue.

Foreign Language
It is any language other than the native language or mother tongue. A foreign language is usually learned not by interaction with others in childhood, but by formal language teaching.

Fossilization
Selinker (1972) noted that most L2 learners fail to reach L2 competence. That is, they stop learning when their internalized rule system contains rules different from those of the L2. This is referred to as 'fossilization'.

Habit-formation
According to the behaviorist view of first language acquisition, children form habits of the language they acquire by a continuous imitation of sounds and patterns of the adults and older children around them. They receive encouragement from those in the environment around them to continue the process of imitation until these children form "habits" of correct language use. The use of these forms becomes automatic for them to use freely.

Imitation
It refers to the child's behavior in copying the language he has around him. The importance of the notion is twofold. First, it has been shown that imitation cannot by itself account for the facts of language development (despite a popular view to the contrary – that children learn language by imitating their parents). Forms such as *mouses and *goed, and sentences such as *Me not like that, show that some internal process of construction is taking place. Secondly, the skills a child shows when he is actually imitating are often different, in important aspects, from those he displays in spontaneous speech production, or in comprehension.

Individual Learner Differences
It refers to the differences in how learners learn an L2, how fast they learn, and how successful they are. These differences include both general factors, such as language learning aptitude and motivation, and specific learner strategies. The differences can be cognitive, affective, or social in nature.

Innate(ness)
It refers to the view that a child is born with a biological predisposition to learn language. The innateness hypothesis argues that the rapid and complex development of children's grammatical competence can be explained only by the hypothesis that they are born with an innate knowledge of at least some of the universal structural principles of human language. This view has received considerable support in generative linguistics, but controversy abounds over the nature of the early linguistic knowledge which might be attributable to the child, and whether this knowledge can be specified independently of other (e.g. cognitive) factors.

Input
The input constitutes the language to which the leaner is exposed. It can be spoken or written. Input serves as the data which the learner must use to determine the rules of the L2.

Intelligence
It is the general mental ability to master academic skills in the form of seeing, learning, understanding and knowing.

Interference
Interference in SLA refers to old habits which get in the way of learning new habits. Thus, the patterns of the learner's L1 get in the way of learning the patterns of the L2.

Interlanguage (IL)
It is the type of language produced by L2 learners. Errors in the learner's language are caused by several processes which include; L1 transfer, overgeneralization, strategies in learning and communication, and transfer of training. The learner's language as a result of these processes

differ from both the L1 and the L2 and it is termed as the learner's interlanguage system.

Internalization
Refers to a process whereby L2 learners come to process knowledge of the structure of the L2, e.g. when these learners make such errors as *mans* and *mouses*, they show that a plural formation rule has been internalized or acquired.

Language Acquisition
Several stages can be distinguished in the chronological development of the native language in children, although the processes leading from the 'prelinguistic' to the 'linguistic' stages are continuous, and there may be considerable individual variation.

Language Acquisition Device
Linguists and psychologists study the process of language learning by comparing input with output, i.e. by comparing the language an infant is exposed to with the language an infant produces. Exactly how the brain acquires language competence is not known, but the term Language Acquisition Device, often abbreviated L.A.D., is applied to the unknown quantity in the model roughly below:

$$\text{input} \longrightarrow \boxed{\text{L. A. D.}} \longrightarrow \text{output}$$

Lexicography
A branch of applied lexicology, concerned with the principles and practice of dictionary-making, i.e. compiling, comparing, defining and grouping lexical items in a book form.

Metacognitive Strategies
Many L2 learners are able to think consciously about how they learn and how successfully they are learning. Metacognitive strategies involve planning learning, monitoring the process of learning, and evaluating how successful a particular strategy is.

Mistakes
They are made by a learner in writing or speaking as a result of inattention, fatigue, carelessness, or some other aspects of performance.

Mistakes appear in form of 'false starts', repeats, corrections and slips of the tongue.

Motivation
Motivation means the factors that determine a person's desire to do something. Two types of motivation are distinguished, 'instrumental motivation', which occurs when the learner's goal is functional (e.g. to get a job or pass an examination), and 'integrative motivation', which occurs when the learner wishes to identify with the culture of the L2 group.

Natural Environment
The linguistic environment refers to those features of the external world in relation to which an utterance or text has meaning. The natural environment refers to the atmosphere around the learner where he or she hears the language uttered by native speakers.

Natural Language
Natural language is the native tongue of a human speech community, such as Arabic or English, as opposed to artificial languages such as Esperanto or ALGOL.

Neurolinguistics
A branch of linguistics, sometimes called neurological linguistics, which studies the neurological basis of language development and use in humans, and attempts to construct a model of the brain's control over the processes of speech and hearing. The main approach has been to postulate the stages of a 'neural program', which would explain the observed phenomena of temporal articulatory co-ordination, sequencing, and other features of speech production. Central to this approach has been the research findings from two main areas: the study of clinical linguistic conditions (such as aphasia and stuttering), in an attempt to deduce the nature of the underlying system from the analysis of its various stages of breakdown; and the study of speech production in parametric articulatory phonetic terms – especially of the 'normal' errors which are introduced into speech (e.g. tongue-slips and hesitations).

Overgeneralization
A process common in both first – and second – language learning, in which a learner extends the use of a grammatical rule or linguistic item beyond its accepted uses, generally by making words or structures follow a more regular pattern. For example, a child or a learner uses **mans* instead of *men* for the plural of 'man' or 'comed' instead of 'came' for the regular Past Tense.

Perception
The recognition and understanding of events, objects, and stimuli through the use of sense (sight, hearing, touch, etc.).

Pragmatics
The study of the use of language in communication, particularly the relationships between sentences and contexts in which they are used. It is sometimes contrasted with 'semantics', which deals with meaning without reference to the users and communicative functions of sentences.

Proficiency
Proficiency consists of the learner's knowledge of the L2; it can be considered synonymous with 'competence'. L2 proficiency is usually measured in relation to native-speaker proficiency.

Psycholinguistics
Within the general framework of interdisciplinary studies concerned with human behavior and language, psycho-linguistics refers to the efforts of both linguists and psychologists to explain whether certain hypotheses about language acquisition and language competence, as proposed by contemporary linguistic theories, have a real basis in terms of perception, memory, intelligence, motivation, etc. This sometimes involves the observation of actual linguistic behavior in laboratory conditions (e.g. word association studies) or the close monitoring of communicative situations (e.g. description of hesitation forms, recall and sentence complexity).

Reinforcement
The act of strengthening or supporting language learning by additional assistance, material or support. This usually refers to the support the child receives from the environment while developing and producing his or her language. It has two types: positive and negative.

Second Language
A language other than one's mother-tongue used for a special purpose, e.g. for education, for government, etc.

Second Language Acquisition (SLA)
SLA is the study of how learners learn an additional language after they have acquired their mother tongue. It refers to the subconscious or conscious processes by which a language other than the mother-tongue is learned in a natural or a tutored setting. It covers the development of phonology, lexis, grammar, and pragmatic knowledge. The study of SLA is directed at accounting for the learner's competence, but in order to do so, it has been set out to investigate empirically how a learner performs when he or she uses a second language.

Self-esteem
Self-esteem relates to having a good opinion of oneself.

Social Strategies
These are one type of learning strategies. They concern the ways in which learners elect to interact with other learners and native speakers.

Speech Defect (also Speech Disorder)
Any abnormality in the production of speech which interferes with communication, such as aphasia or stuttering.

Speech Therapy/Pathology
Treatment for the elimination and/or alleviation of speech and language disorders. The treatment is carried out by speech therapists in collaboration with doctors, psychologists and occasionally linguists. The alternative term to speech pathology is clinical linguistics.

Stammering or Stuttering
Stammering or stuttering is a speech impediment, usually due to psycho-physiological disturbances and is more frequent in male than female speakers, in which consonant sounds and syllables are spasmodically repeated, particularly at the beginning of words.

Strategy
Procedures used in learning, thinking, etc, which serve as a way of reaching a goal. In language learning, learning strategies (e.g. generalization and inferencing) and communication strategies (e.g. paraphrase, gesture and mime) are those conscious or unconscious processes which language learners make use of in learning and using a language.

Stylistics
Stylistics is the application of linguistic knowledge to the study of style. Traditionally, stylistic analysis has been mainly concerned with the analysis of literary style or the language variety characteristic of a writer. Various criteria have been set up to deal with individual or group styles in relation to biographical, psychological, social and other details reflecting the personality of its creator. More recently, emphasis has shifted to the linguistic description of the utterance itself in terms of its components and characteristic 'deviations' from the standard language, and also to a widening of the notion of style within the framework of variety studies.

Surface Structure
It is generally the syntactic structure of the sentence which a person speaks, hears, reads or writes.

Theoretical Linguistics
In so far as the subject attempts to establish general principles for the study of all languages, and to determine the characteristics of human language as a phenomenon, it may be called general linguistics or theoretical linguistics.

Transfer
Transfer is the process of using knowledge of the first language in learning a second language. Transfer can be positive when a first language

pattern identical with a target or second language pattern is transferred. It can also be negative when a first language pattern different from the target or second language pattern is transferred. In the latter case, the L1 may promote errors to occur.

Transformation
It is the part of Generative Transformation Grammar that contains the transformational rules: deletion, movement, substitution and insertion. These rules change a basic syntactic structure (i.e. deep structure) into a sentence-like structure (i.e. surface structure).

Transitional Competence
This is the term used by Corder (1967) to refer to interim rule systems that learners develop in the process of SLA.

Universal Grammar (UG)
One meaning of universal grammar concerns aspects of language found in many languages, called statistical, typological or 'Greenbergian' universals, for instance, word- order correlation and the accessibility hierarchy for relative clauses. The meaning of universal grammar (UG) within Chomskyan theories is the language faculty – the aspects of language built into the mind that become knowledge of a particular grammar when exposed to language input. UG theory explores the nature of language knowledge and of acquisition in both L1 and L2. Since the mid-eighties, UG has been identified with the Principles and Parameters Theory.

Utterance
Utterence is what is said by one person before or after another person begins to speak. An utterance may consist of a word, one sentence or more.

Verbal Contact
It is using a language as a means of communication or interacting with the people who use this language as first language.

Whole/Part-skill Performance
During the SLA process, learners have to learn and perfect an extremely complicated set of skills to achieve full fluency. These skills are of two types: whole skills and part skills. Whole-skills refer to the correct response to a verbal or written stimulus, the use of appropriate grammatical patterns and vocabulary, translating from one language into another, etc. Part-skills refer to identification and recognition, control of articulatory and graphic processes, and vocabulary.

Appendix

Arabic Phonemes

Consonants

No	Description	SA*	Arabic
1	voiced bilabial plosive	b	ب
2	voiceless denti-alveolar plosive	t	ت
3	voiceless pharyngealizeddenti-alveolar plosive	tˤ	ط
4	voiced denti-alveolar plosive	d	د
5	voiceless velar plosive	k	ك
6	voiceless velar plosive	dʒ	ج
7	voiceless uvular plosive	q	ق
8	voiceless glottal stop	ʔ	ء
9	voiced pharyngealizeddenti-alveolar plosive	dˤ	ض
10	voiced bilabial nasal	m	م
11	voiced denti-alveolar nasal	n	ن
12	voiceless labiodental fricative	f	ف
13	voiceless dental fricative	θ	ث
14	voiced dental fricative	ð	ذ
15	voiced pharyngealized dental fricative	ðˤ	ظ
16	voiceless alveolar fricative	s	س
17	voiceless pharyngealized alveolar fricative	sˤ	ص
18	voiced alveolar fricative	z	ز
19	voiceless postalveolar fricative	ʃ	ش
20	voiceless uvular fricative	χ	خ
21	voiced uvular fricative	ʁ	غ

No	Description	SA*	Arabic
22	voiceless pharyngeal fricative	ħ	ح
23	voiced pharyngeal fricative	ʕ	ع
24	voiceless glottal fricative	h	ه
25	voiced alveolar trill	r	ر
26	voiced alveolar lateral	l	ل
27	voiced palatal approximant	j	ي
28	voiced labio-velar approximant	w	و

* SA: Standard Arabic

Vowels

No	Description	SA*	Arabic
1	low central short unrounded	a	ـَ الفتحة
2	low central long unrounded	a:	الألف الممدودة
3	high front short unrounded	ɪ	ـِ الكسرة
4	high front long unrounded	i:	الياء الممدودة
5	high back short rounded	ʊ	ـُ الضمة
6	high back long rounded	u:	الواو الممدودة

* SA: Standard Arabic

www.ingramcontent.com/pod-product-compliance
Ingram Content Group UK Ltd.
Pitfield, Milton Keynes, MK11 3LW, UK
UKHW020857160426
5217IPUK00039B/1240

9 783034 321112